Revisiting
The Reading Workshop

Management, Mini-Lessons, and Strategies

A Complete Guide to Organizing and Managing an Effective
Reading Workshop That Builds Independent, Strategic Readers

by Barbara Orehovec and Marybeth Alley

SCHOLASTIC
PROFESSIONAL BOOKS

NEW YORK • TORONTO • LONDON • AUCKLAND • SYDNEY
MEXICO CITY • NEW DELHI • HONG KONG • BUENOS AIRES

DEDICATION

For our families—

To our parents, Nancy and Joe and Maryjane and Jerry,
who made certain that we knew the beautiful princesses, handsome princes,
and big ugly giants within so many storybooks.
With their guidance, we learned how to love a good story.

And to our husbands, John and Jason,
who remind us daily that we can, indeed, live happily ever after.
With their support, we've learned to teach our students how to love a good story.

ACKNOWLEDGMENTS

In true collaborative fashion, this book would not have come to be without the talents, interest, support, ideas, and inspiration of a great many people. We are most thankful to:

Our students, who made this book possible. By inviting us into their reading lives each and every day, they have taught us how to help them. They are the true stars of this book.

Our many colleagues at James River Elementary and throughout the Williamsburg-James City County School Division. So many teachers have opened their minds and their classroom doors to us throughout the development of this book. This strong support system allowed and encouraged us to tell our story.

Our principal, Lucia Sebastian, who never for a second doubted our ability to see this project through. As an administrator who immediately recognized the strength of the Reading Workshop, she encouraged and supported its implementation throughout our school, our school division, as well as throughout the state.

Our editors at Scholastic. Wendy Murray and Joanna Davis-Swing recognized the need to take teachers into our school to show them a real Reading Workshop. Merryl Maleska Wilbur provided the guidance and insight to strengthen this finished product. And our designer, Jackie Swensen, made our ideas come alive.

Cover design by Josué Castilleja
Cover photo by SODA
Interior design by Solutions by Design, Inc.
Interior photos courtesy of the authors

ISBN: 0-439-44404-7

Copyright 2003 by Barbara Orehovec and Marybeth Alley.
All rights reserved. Printed in the USA.

6 7 8 9 10   40   09 08 07 06 05

TABLE OF
CONTENTS

Introduction 7

CHAPTER ONE
ESTABLISHING A LITERATE COMMUNITY:
Basic Elements of a Reading Workshop 9

   Defining the Elements of a Reading Workshop 10

      The Mini-Lesson and Read Aloud 10

      Independent Reading and Conferring 12

      Response and Reflection 12

      Sharing 13

   Rationale and Support for a Reading Workshop 13

   The Reading Workshop Classroom vs. Traditional Practices 15

CHAPTER TWO
SETTING THE STAGE:
Organization and Management of the Reading Workshop 17

   **Be Prepared: Know Your Reasons and Your Expectations as You Establish
      Your Own Reading Workshop** 18

   Three Top Priorities for Your Workshop 19

      Encouraging "On-task" Behaviors 19

      Scheduling the Time 21

      Planning Your Classroom Space 22

   Set Up the Classroom Library 23

      Seek Out Sources for Books 23

      Organize Your Literature Collection for Optimal Student Use 24

      Establish a Book Checkout System 27

   Invite Students and Parents into the Workshop "Community" 29

      Provide Book Nooks for Independent Reading Time 30

      Organize Records and Reading Materials 30

      Create a Reading Workshop Companion Book 31

      Keep Parents Informed 32

CHAPTER THREE
PREPARING TO TEACH:
How to Plan for and Structure Successful Mini-Lessons 37
Planning Mini-Lessons 38
A Recommended Planning Form 39
Long-term and Short-term Planning 39
Good Plans Lead to Expected and Unexpected Instruction 43
Structuring the Mini-Lesson 44
Teacher-Directed Instruction 44
Student Responsibility During Mini-Lessons 44
Ideas for Involving Students 44
Ending the Mini-Lesson 47
Ensuring a Smooth Transition to Independent Reading 48

CHAPTER FOUR
ESTABLISHING ROUTINES:
Mini-Lessons on Procedures 51
September Is a Special Month in the Reading Workshop 52
Four Weeks of Lessons to Phase In the Reading Workshop 52
Sample Procedural Mini-Lesson on Selecting a Book Nook 55
Twenty Days of Mini-Lessons 56
Favorite Book Sharing 57
What Good Listeners Do 57
Our Reading Workshop: An Introduction 58
Introduction to Quiet Reading and Book Nooks 58
Reading Workshop Rules 58
Caring for Books and the Classroom Library 58
Appropriate Workshop Voices 59
Choosing a Just Right Book 59
Mapping out Book Nooks 60
Strategies for Choosing Books 60
Reading Conferences 61
Help Me 61
Reading Workshop Office Work 61
Possible Book Responses and Journal Writing 62
Share Time 63
Giving a Book Talk 63
Bringing All the Pieces Together/Trouble Shooting 63
Reading With a Partner 64
The (Right) Way to Have a Reading Workshop 64

CHAPTER FIVE
PURSUING MEANING:
Mini-Lessons on Reading Strategies and Skills. 65

Reading Strategies and Skills Instruction. 66

The Importance of Mini-Lessons on Reading Strategies and Skills 66

Mini-Lesson Lesson Plan for Strategy and Skill Instruction. 67

Developing Mini-Lessons on Reading Comprehension Strategies 68

Topics for Mini-Lessons on Reading Strategies. 68

Recommended Books for Mini-Lessons on Reading Strategies 68

Extended Sample Reading Strategy Mini-Lesson: Making Connections from
Text to Self 69

Eight Key Reading Strategy Lesson Plans 73

Developing Mini-Lessons on Reading Skills 85

Topics for Mini-Lessons on Reading Skills 85

Recommended Books for Mini-Lessons on Reading Skills 85

Extended Sample Reading Skill Mini-Lesson 87

CHAPTER SIX
EXPLORING THE TEXT:
Mini-Lessons on Literary Elements and Literary Techniques 89

Literary Elements and Literary Techniques Instruction 89

Developing Mini-Lessons on Literary Elements 91

Topics for Mini-Lessons on Literary Elements 91

Recommended Books for Mini-Lessons on Literary Elements. 92

Extended Sample Literary Elements Mini-Lesson 93

Developing Mini-Lessons on Literary Techniques 95

Topics for Mini-Lessons on Literary Techniques. 95

Recommended Books for Mini-Lessons on Literary Techniques 96

Sample Literary Techniques Mini-Lesson 97

CHAPTER SEVEN
READING AS REAL READERS:
Independent Reading, Conferring, Responding, and Sharing 99

Independent Reading: Behaviors and Practices 99

Sharing Your Own Passion for Reading 100

Orderly Environment 100

Book Choice. 100

Reading With Others 101

Story Chats. 102

Guided Reading 103

Flexible Grouping. 105

Conferring With Students: "How's It Going?" 106

What a Conference Looks and Feels Like 106

Three-Part Model 109

Keeping Track 109

Different Times for Conferring 109

Different Types of Conferences 109

Teacher Interventions for Students With Reading Difficulties 112

Two Extended Sample Reading Conferences 115

Responding and Sharing 118

Conversations About Reading 118

Responding Through Writing 119

Sharing 123

CHAPTER EIGHT

INFORMING INSTRUCTION:

Effective Assessment in the Reading Workshop 125

Matching Readers With Books 126

Listening to Students' Reading 126

Student Interviews 126

Pulling Up a Chair: Procedures for Ongoing Observation of Students' Reading 130

Opportunities for Observation and Assessment in a Reading Workshop 130

Anecdotal Records 130

Observational Checklists 133

Running Records 136

Informal Error Analysis 137

Oral Retellings 137

Written Retellings 138

Reading Logs 138

Journal Responses 139

Evaluating Progress 139

Semester End Reading Inventory 139

Rubrics 140

Communication 146

Recommended Children's Literature for Your Reading Workshop 149

Professional Resources 155

Appendices 156

"SHHH! WE ARE READING," THE HANDWRITTEN SIGN ON THE OUTSIDE OF THE CLASSROOM door beckons you to enter, to take a look for yourself, to remember what it is that you love about reading. Two or three students whisper to each other in the classroom library; their private giggles result in a decision—they'll read this next book together as partners. Open books and little bodies are sprinkled on the floor. Readers are hard at work—lying on their bellies, backs against a wall, curled up in beanbag chairs, up close to a reading buddy, all over the room. A small group of four students huddles in a corner, seriously debating why an author chose such an ending for a story. A teacher shares a reading with one student, coaching the young reader through the new text. Two students are taking notes from their non-fiction reading in a notebook. The room is not noisy, it is alive. It is not chaotic; it is inviting. You're just about to question how this atmosphere has come to be when the answer actually finds you. You've only been in the room for a matter of moments, but someone has spotted you. A small hand takes hold of your arm and begins pulling at your sleeve. "Hurry," he says, "this is the good part. Come read with me!"

Our Reading Workshops are dynamic, stimulating places. Our students have ample time to engage in authentic reading experiences. They are learning to act as we do, as real readers do. They value personal judgments, comfy places, friendly recommendations, and informed choices. They respond, reflect, and discuss their reading. They read for real reasons.

As with any worthwhile undertaking, the Reading Workshop we refer to here was not created overnight. The seeds for our Workshop approach were planted amid the frustration of not doing enough for all the varying student needs, of not setting aside enough time for reading and reflection, of not helping all of our students reach their greatest potential. In many ways, the development of our Reading Workshop was a slow process, changing bit by bit over the years. Yet in many ways, we witnessed dramatic changes very quickly in our young readers. We experimented, tweaked, failed, succeeded, changed, added, and created.

Throughout the entire creation process, we constantly returned to the notion of how we, as readers, behave. We choose where we read, and comfortable places always win out. More often than not, we choose what we will read. We abandon books that aren't enjoyable. We reflect on our reading, creating our own literary tastes. We enjoy the chance to talk about books with friends and relatives. We relish being part of a literate community.

This book developed out of our collaborative efforts to provide all of our students with rich, meaningful, authentic reading experiences. Barbara's expertise as our school's Reading Specialist has shaped much of the underlying philosophy of the Reading Workshop. Marybeth's classroom experiences have given the Workshop a tried and true authenticity. What began as a collaborative effort in one second-grade classroom has since grown to a Reading Workshop program in many classrooms, in many schools, from first through fifth grade.

As word spread and more teachers began to share in the remarkable experiences of a Reading Workshop classroom, we realized teachers needed help getting a Workshop off the ground and maintaining it. Fellow colleagues wanted as much information as we could give them about Reading Workshops. They were interested in the books we used for read-alouds, how we determined the focus of our mini-lessons, how we managed and organized the workshop, and how we met the needs of all students while at the same time fostering independence.

It is our sincerest hope that this book will provide teachers with what they have asked for: a practical way to build and enjoy the Reading Workshop in their own elementary classrooms. We invite you to create an authentic reading environment for all of your students. We're here now to take hold of your arm, and pull on your sleeve. "Hurry, this is the good part. Come read with us!"

Happy Reading,

Marybeth Alley and Barbara Orehovec

CHAPTER 1

ESTABLISHING A LITERATE COMMUNITY:

Basic Elements of a Reading Workshop

> "I like Reading Workshop because all of the students can read books they want to read."
>
> —Winston, grade 2

The Reading Workshop model offers students time to read, choices about what they will read, and opportunities for conversations about their reading. When you think about it, this is precisely what adults do in their own reading lives. We feel it's not only right but necessary to create the same conditions for our students. Thus, our Reading Workshop provides students with a supportive environment that involves them in authentic reading experiences that focus on the strengths and needs of each individual student. By modeling reading behaviors, providing direct instruction that focuses on strategic reading, and giving our students time to practice being "real readers," we are able to provide dynamic reading experiences for all of our students.

In our roles as classroom teacher and reading specialist, we have been working with the Reading Workshop model for many years, continually fine tuning and personalizing it to fit our own teaching style and the needs of our students. When the new things we try out in our Workshop work well and we witness our students being successful and reading more than ever, we build these new elements into the Workshop model. In this way, we have incorporated the sharing of rich literature, the magic of read alouds, and the power of well-constructed mini-lessons into the basic Reading Workshop model. It is our hope that through this book we will be able to share with you our instructional style and let you in on the wonderful literature we have discovered so that your students' reading, too, can mature and develop within a thoughtfully-crafted Reading Workshop.

In the chapters that follow, we will discuss the specific Workshop components in detail and will demonstrate how you can get the Workshop running smoothly in your classroom. But first, it makes sense to take an overall look at the Reading Workshop.

Defining the Elements of a Reading Workshop

The basic elements of a Reading Workshop are:

- the mini-lesson and read aloud.
- independent reading and conferring.
- response and reflection.
- sharing.

Let's briefly examine each of these elements.

The Mini-Lesson and Read Aloud

A Reading Workshop begins with a 10- to 15-minute **mini-lesson** that teaches concepts, techniques, and strategies while encouraging students to interact with good literature. Mini-lessons can be taught in conjunction with a read aloud. You can use literature to model reading strategies, to discuss literary elements or an author's craft, or to focus on a particular skill such as cause-and-effect relationships. Because this is the most dedicated instructional phase of the Workshop, it is a pivotal time—it is your opportunity to provide direct instruction on the skills and strategies at hand. It is also the time for thoughtful discussion to help students become aware of what expert readers do throughout the reading process. The over-arching goal of the mini-lesson and read aloud is to encourage students to enjoy literature while at the same time increasing their awareness of strategic reading. Read aloud time provides the opportunity for you to share information and to foster students' active listening and engagement with the text.

Because the most effective Reading Workshop lessons are a result of "kid-watching"—close observations of your class—your daily interactions with your students will help you determine the topic of each day's mini-lesson. By carefully observing them as they read and interact with print, you can determine the specific lessons to teach. The mini-lesson provides students with time to listen to good literature, and also offers them the opportunity to listen to and respond to the ideas of others. As you prepare students to engage with the text, to listen to and value the perspectives of others, and to develop their own literary appreciation, you assist students with independent reading, the next component of a Reading Workshop.

> **TEACHER to TEACHER**
> Throughout this book you will find lists of excellent children's literature to use for mini-lessons. In addition, the Appendix, p. 160, has a form that you can complete to help you keep track of the lessons you have taught and the literature you have used.

IMPORTANCE OF READING ALOUD

"The single most important activity for building the knowledge required for eventual success in reading is reading aloud to children."

—Anderson, *Becoming a Nation of Readers*, 1985

Reading aloud provides teachers with incredible opportunities to build a classroom community. As we read aloud to our students, we expose them to a variety of genre, authors, and titles. Students need to have the experience of listening to the best children's literature. They need to hear the beautiful language of books, to get lost in the stories as they explore new places, and to develop the desire to pick up, finish, and reread the books we read to them.

Jim Trelease has written several books on reading aloud to children. In the fourth edition of *The Read-Aloud Handbook* (1995, p. 8), he states: "We read to children for all the same reasons you talk with children: to reassure, to entertain, to inform or explain, to arouse curiosity, to inspire. But in reading aloud, you also:

- condition the child to associate reading with pleasure;
- create background knowledge;
- and provide a reading role model."

There is such power in reading aloud to children. Not only do children hear fluent oral reading, but it gives us an opportunity to share our reading habits and values. Students need to be aware that the time we set aside for reading aloud is important. They also need to know our reasons for choosing particular books. A book may be selected because it complements the curriculum, because it is a "must-read" book that is too challenging for students to read independently, or because it is just enjoyable. This is also a time when we can show students the value of talking about books, of reacting to and responding to literature. By involving students in these conversations, we can encourage their continued dialogue.

Reading aloud is a great way to demonstrate strategic reading practices. We can model for students our thinking processes as we read, such as when we deliberately stop to point out questions we have:

> "That doesn't make sense, I'd better go back and re-read it."

> "Something's not right. I thought the author said the grandfather is sick in bed, but yet he's standing there looking out the window."

By showing them connections we are making with the text, we can encourage their doing so in their own reading:

> "That reminds me of the time Dad and I got up real early at camp and went fishing, just the two of us."

> "This book reminds me of the one we read yesterday, because that family was also homeless."

In this way, we can help students make connections to their own lives, to other books, and to real-world issues. While it is important to model reading strategies during read aloud time, we must also provide students with opportunities for response. Since we want our students to respond to their own reading, we can first have them respond to our read aloud. As Lucy Calkins stated (2000), "Children must first listen and build the world of the story in their minds." We want our students to have that sense of story, but we also realize that not all students are active listeners and may have difficulty visualizing and understanding what is being read to them. These same students are probably the ones who struggle when they attempt to read the text themselves. By providing students with opportunities to respond to our read alouds, we can assist them in responding to their own independent reading as well as responding to reading through conversations with others.

By establishing this reading community as we engage children in read alouds, we help them develop a love of books and an awareness of the value of being a reader.

Independent Reading and Conferring

After the mini-lesson, students engage in **independent reading**. Independent reading lies at the heart of the Reading Workshop, because this is when students work at and practice their reading. They may read alone, in pairs, or in small response groups.

During independent reading time, you have a great opportunity to respond to students' needs and to actively engage in **conferring** with individuals or small groups of students. Or you may spend further time teaching a guided reading lesson or having a small-group lesson on a specific strategy or skill.

Here is a sampling of some possible student activities:

- Participate in a teacher-led guided reading group.

- Engage in a "story chat" with a group of peers.

- Use this time to choose a book or to help another child choose a book.

- Write a response to what they have just finished reading.

Depending upon the kinds of groups you have set up, your instructional goals, and your students' needs, the time you allow for this phase can be quite flexible, varying from 30–60 minutes.

The independent reading segment of the Workshop is also one of your best opportunities for assessment. You can use running records, retellings, or comprehension checks quite naturally during this time. These ongoing informal assessments are vital, as they provide you with the information you need to plan for future instruction. Chapter 8 covers the Reading Workshop assessment process in detail.

Response and Reflection

Students benefit from opportunities to **respond and reflect** about what they're reading. Conversations with the teacher or with other students at the start of reading, during reading, or after completing a book help students clarify their thinking, ponder questions, and develop divergent thinking. Younger children may need a designated time period at the end of independent reading in which they are specifically directed to write.

There are many different possibilities for response. Students may:

- share connections they made to the day's mini-lesson or to their own personal lives.

- keep their journals with them and write their responses and reactions while they are reading.

- log the books they have read and write in response to directions by the teacher—for example, a summary of what was read or a statement of their favorite part of their reading.

- engage in a more personal response to their reading by describing connections to their own lives.

These verbal and written responses offer ways to engage your students while providing you with substantial information for assessment and evaluation.

Sharing

After the reading and reflection period, students come together again for about five or ten minutes of **share** time. The teacher leads the students as they describe their reading successes to one another. For example, students might:

- 📖 give a brief book talk and recommend a book to their classmates.

- 📖 discuss their reactions to a piece of literature.

- 📖 share what occurred during a small group book discussion.

These activities let students engage in a forum for sharing their enthusiasm of literature and for listening to and appreciating the ideas of others.

As the teacher, you can use this time to provide a connection to the day's mini-lesson. In this way you can determine your students' level of understanding of your focused lesson.

Rationale and Support for a Reading Workshop

There is a great deal of support for the Workshop model from many leaders in the field of reading instruction.

Nancie Atwell's book, *In the Middle* (1999), first published in 1987, changed the way of thinking about how reading is taught. In working with middle-school students, Atwell realized that her own reading habits didn't match her teaching practices. As someone who enjoyed reading and discussing literature with family and friends, she knew that she needed to create similar opportunities for her students. She found her answer within the structure of the Reading Workshop; within this framework she could offer her students far longer time blocks for independent reading than within a traditional classroom instructional setting. She could also provide her students with a rich variety of literature from which they could make their own selections. Additionally, her students could regularly meet and engage in real "reader-to-reader dialogue" among themselves, thereby furthering their understanding and interest in the books they read.

Lucy Calkins, well known for her work with the Writing Workshop and the author of *The Art of Teaching Writing* (1994), has recently expanded her expertise into reading. After working closely with teachers and students in the New York City schools, she wrote *The Art of Teaching Reading* (2001). In it she points out that students need to have meaningful literary experiences so that they can "compose richly literate lives." In order for students to become successful readers, they must read frequently and they must read for extended periods of time. The independent reading component of a Reading Workshop, which Calkins feels is its most important element, provides this opportunity for students. Calkins also believes that students must be given decision-making power about what they will read. In order to meet these goals, fully-stocked and well-developed classroom libraries—offering both rich sets of literature and multi-grade leveled books—are essential.

Richard Allington also feels that students need increased time to engage in real reading. He pointed out in 1994 that, although American children were reading more than they had ten years earlier, they were still spending less than ten percent of the school day involved in actual reading and writing. In his book, *What Really Matters for Struggling Readers* (2001), he furthers this point by describing how neither struggling nor capable readers are best served by limited time for real reading. The problem is manifested in several ways—capable readers, who need time to "get lost in a book"—are often instead required to spend four to six weeks on a whole-class novel. At the same time, struggling readers simply need the experience of independent reading time; too often their classroom reading time is spent exclusively in lessons with the teacher.

At the 2000 Southeast Regional International Reading Association (IRA) conference in Savannah, GA, Allington stated that the only effective ways to improve reading achievement are to:

📖 increase actual reading and writing activity.

📖 select more appropriate literacy texts and tasks.

📖 enhance useful strategy instruction.

Allington's book (2001) addresses these concerns:

1. In order to provide more time for reading and writing, he calls for large blocks of uninterrupted time. The school day may need to be reorganized to provide this.

2. He promotes "thoughtful literacy instruction" where students think about what they've read and explain their thinking. In this way, the students move beyond the mere act of remembering material to truly understanding it.

3. In order for this understanding to develop, students need strategy instruction to help them learn to summarize, analyze, and synthesize material. Teachers may need to rethink their teaching so they can provide the necessary ongoing strategy instruction.

4. Another critical component of solid reading instruction involves "literate conversations" among students. Teachers can foster dialogue by providing modeling and time for students to talk with them and with peers about books and about reading strategies.

Carol Avery, in her 1993 book, *And With a Light Touch*, describes how children at the earliest levels benefit from a workshop approach to reading. Realizing that students need lots of time to read, she builds in concerted blocks of real reading time for her first graders. She provides choices in reading material by including a variety of genres and reading levels in her classroom library. She believes that when students learn to make choices they "choose to read outside of school as well as within the workshop." She also insures time for her students to interact with each other about books. These interactions help the students see what "real reading" is all about.

Avery believes that teachers can meet the diverse needs of students in a workshop by considering their interests, experiences, and learning styles. As she worked with her students in the Reading Workshop, she realized that "No two children learn to read with the same timing and with identical strategies. No two readers appreciate the same reading material or read at the same pace" (p. 337).

The underlying message emerging from all of these researchers and educators is that teachers must put real reading behaviors at the heart of teaching practices. A Reading Workshop will help you set up an effective framework in which to accomplish this, as well as to meet the needs of your diverse students.

The Reading Workshop Classroom vs. Traditional Practices

A Reading Workshop classroom is an interactive, busy place. Students share the responsibility for their learning as they make book choices and decide how they will respond to the literature they are reading. The teacher meets the needs of students individually and in groups. Even as she is addressing these needs, she is observing and assessing what is needed next for instruction.

In many ways, there are explicit, discernible differences between a Reading Workshop classroom and a classroom organized around more traditional literacy teaching practices. The following chart compares the two approaches by highlighting five essential components of an overall reading program. It is our opinion that students who are learning to read in a Reading Workshop environment have access to many enhanced forms of literacy instruction not available otherwise.

COMPARING THE TRADITIONAL AND READING WORKSHOP APPROACHES

TRADITIONAL	READING WORKSHOP
TIME FOR READING	
Limited	Increased
◆ Reading group or whole class reading	◆ Students involved in independent reading
◆ Students may only be reading during their reading group.	◆ Students read during the entire Reading Workshop.
◆ Students given "seatwork" when not in reading group	◆ Students read independently, in pairs, and in small groups.
◆ Students "held back" in reading; i.e., teacher has all students reading at same pace	◆ Students read at their own pace; they can move ahead or re-read as necessary.
DIRECT INSTRUCTION	
Tasks and Skills Emphasized	Strategic Reading Emphasized
◆ Reading is taught as a task to complete.	◆ Reading is taught as a process with teacher modeling strategies.
◆ Primary instruction on reading skills in a sequential format	◆ Instruction emphasizes reading strategies through literature and based on need.
◆ Less interesting, less challenging instruction provided to less able readers	◆ Higher-level instruction provided to all readers
◆ Students not aware of teacher's reading processes and practices	◆ Teacher models reading processes and shares reading practices (use of read alouds and think alouds, demonstrations).

TRADITIONAL	READING WORKSHOP

INSTRUCTIONAL PRACTICES

Teacher-driven	Student-centered
◈ Students are grouped by reading ability.	◈ Students may be grouped by level, by interest, or in flexible need-based groups.
◈ Round-robin oral reading is practiced.	◈ Silent and oral reading; discussion with teachers and/or students
◈ Vocabulary instruction presented in a list format to learn	◈ Vocabulary learned incidentally through reading material
◈ Teacher makes all decisions.	◈ Student has ownership and responsibility for: choosing books, reading independently, using strategies, preparing for conferences.
◈ Teacher selects reading materials for individuals and groups.	◈ Students choose (with guidance) their reading material.
◈ Students perceive themselves as part of one reading group.	◈ Students are part of a whole-class reading community.

OPPORTUNITIES FOR RESPONSE

Receptive	Interactive
◈ Teacher responds to students.	◈ Students have conversations with other students as well as with the teacher.
◈ Few writing opportunities	◈ Writing occurs before, during, and after reading.

RELATIONSHIP OF ASSESSMENT TO INSTRUCTION

Test-Taking Dominates	Assessment Informs Instruction
◈ Students assessed in typical test-taking format: read book and answer questions; multiple-choice format	◈ Students involved in alternative forms of assessment: anecdotal records, running records, journals, observations, checklists, rubrics, conferences
◈ All students assessed in the same manner	◈ Ongoing assessments and observations of individual students to determine their strengths and weaknesses
◈ Teacher follows set guidelines in a prescribed sequence.	◈ Teacher makes instructional decisions based on assessment.

CHAPTER 2

SETTING THE STAGE:

Organization and Management of the Reading Workshop

> "I know where everything belongs, so I don't have to bother anyone when I need something for my reading."
>
> —Meagan, grade 3

A s you might expect, there's much more to establishing an effective Reading Workshop than just knowing what the major components are. The next step involves being able to visualize the Workshop running smoothly in your room. Before diving into the nitty-gritty of organization, let's take a peek into a Reading Workshop classroom, a classroom where careful attention has been paid to organization and management.

An untrained non-educator visiting this room would probably be mildly impressed with the soft tones, the unorthodox seating arrangements, and the generally relaxed yet productive atmosphere (see "A Working Workshop," page 18). A teacher who knows what it takes to keep students on task when she is not working directly with them would be wowed!

Obviously, this kind of smooth Workshop routine did not happen overnight. In fact, it probably didn't even happen in just a couple of weeks. And it certainly didn't happen just because the teacher taught a mini-lesson, set up some independent reading time, and gathered the group for a final share time. It happened because the teacher was prepared. It happened because the teacher was constantly thinking. And it happened because the teacher knew what she wanted out of her Reading Workshop.

In this chapter, we provide you with many of the tools necessary to create a similar, effective Workshop in your own classroom. These are the "nuts and bolts" that hold the classroom together, that allow you to conference with only one or two students at a time yet remain confident that the other students in your room, wherever they are, are busy at work, creating their own independent reading lives.

Be Prepared: Know Your Reasons and Your Expectations as You Establish Your Own Reading Workshop

One of the most frequently-asked questions about making the switch to a Reading Workshop format is, "Why?" It's also a question that you need to ask yourself at the get-go. You'll need to be able to verbalize why you see the need for the change to colleagues, to administrators, and perhaps most importantly, to parents. (Luckily, as we saw in Chapter 1, there's lots of research to back you up!) Take the time to sit down and write out a rationale—even if it's only a few sentences. Having a personal rationale will not only keep you focused as you plan the elements of the Workshop, it will also come in handy when those few nay-sayers you know start asking questions or raising eyebrows. When considering your rationale for moving toward the Reading Workshop model, you may want to think about questions such as the following:

- What are you doing in your classroom right now that meshes with the Workshop model?

- What areas of your classroom life would be most affected by the change?

- Do your students already have a large amount of uninterrupted independent reading time?

- Do they have time for thoughtful reflection and sharing?

- Why do you feel learning to be a life-long reader is a necessary skill for all students?

TEACHER to TEACHER

When we began our journey toward the Reading Workshop model for reading instruction, we kept the following rationale in mind: "Our students read now, but we know we can encourage even more reading. We believe students can become real readers who think, talk, and act like literate members of a community. Reading is more than skills and comprehension. Reading is a way of life."

Once you have clarified your own overall goals and rationale, you are ready to pull together a list of more specific expectations. This necessary list will guide you through all of your attempts at organization. Your expectations will serve as a road map to guide you through the many possibilities of running a Workshop. For example, one of your personal expectations might state, "Students will respond to the literature both in speaking and in writing." This tells you that your students will need both time to reflect and certain materials to get their job done. You will need to model and discuss how readers talk about books with other readers. And you will also need to establish a system for your students to write down their thoughts and reactions to books, probably in individual reading journals.

The table on page 20 illustrates one third-grade teacher's expectations and what those expectations meant for her own classroom. Ideas in the left column reflect the teacher's ideology regarding reading instruction. Ideas in the right column reflect changes she will need to incorporate into her classroom to help her students meet the expectations.

Three Top Priorities for Your Workshop

Encouraging "On-task" Behaviors

As you look over your list of expectations, you might notice that you return again and again to the notion of on-task behavior. We've done this, too. When we're honest with ourselves, we all know that in order for the Workshop to succeed, students must remain on task. Your Reading Workshop must look and feel well managed—to the students, to the teacher, and to other visitors to the room.

To accomplish this, you need a "behavior management plan." Although that term often refers to an elaborate system of earnings and deductions, consequences and rewards, it doesn't have to be that complicated or rigid. In fact, in the Workshop, it's important that your "management" is not merely a discipline measure. Management in the Workshop is your way of ensuring that all students are doing all they can to grow in literacy.

Think about the following questions when developing your own plan to ensure engaged, on-task students:

    📖 What can I do to ensure that my students know what to do and that they will, in fact, do it?

    📖 Will I use the same set of rules that guides our general, daily classroom life? Or will I create a new set of rules that applies just to the Reading Workshop?

    📖 Will I write the rules up in advance? Or will we work together as a class to negotiate a list of rules for reading time?

Using your list of expectations, draft a set of rules that will be in effect during each Workshop session. As you create your rules, keep in mind that these guidelines need to set the stage for independent activity. (See page 21 for one sample set of such rules.) Your overall goal should be for students who are not meeting with you in a group or in a conference to be self-sustaining readers and thinkers.

> ### TEACHER to TEACHER
> Introduce students to the Reading Workshop rules at the start and have them keep a copy of these rules with their reading materials. Sending a copy of the rules home to parents during the first week of Workshop implementation is also a smart, pro-active move.

Expectations for a Reading Workshop in my own classroom	Implications for my classroom environment
◆ Students will know that something different is happening at this time and in this place. We are not merely "at school," we are not reviewing for a test or completing a "to-do" list. We are experiencing life and creating literate lives.	◆ An *ambiance*—the room will need a "feel" of literature. It must be clear to everyone who enters the room that reading and literacy are of the greatest importance to us.
◆ Students will read. They will not waste their time. They will read only books that they love.	◆ A *management plan* that convinces kids, "I mean business," because reading is that important to me.
◆ Students will respond to the literature both in speaking and in writing.	◆ *Time* to write and reflect. Directions on how to discuss books with friends.
◆ Students will record the books and genres they are reading or abandoning.	◆ A *reading log sheet.*
◆ Students will read from a variety of genres. They will feel comfortable enough to try new authors and genres.	◆ Plenty of *books* to choose from. Discussions and recommendations among students and teachers.
◆ Students will read for at least one half hour every night.	◆ *Homework monitoring system* that works for me, my students, and parents.
◆ Students will take good care of the books that they borrow from the room. They will return books before checking out new ones.	◆ *Consequences* for lost or damaged books. Easy-to-use check-out system that works for both the students and me.
◆ Students will think, think, think! They will recognize their successes and gladly return for the next workshop. Students will take part in housekeeping in all workshop areas. It is <u>our</u> room, not <u>my</u> room.	◆ Lots of challenges and a predictable *schedule* with just enough unknowns to keep them coming back for more. Clear expectations of how the room should look and simple, logical consequences when expectations are not met.
◆ Students will attempt to solve reading problems on their own at first. They will recall and use strategies for comprehending and decoding.	◆ Lots of *reminders*—bookmarks, charts around the room. Discussions on how to ask peers for help. A system for letting me know I am needed without interrupting a group or conference.
◆ Students will keep a reading journal full of notes, quotations, and responses that remind them of the books they have read.	◆ *Journals* (marbleized composition book); models of other students' journals or my own; and demonstrations on how to keep a journal.
◆ Students will read as much as they possibly can and, in turn, be able to verbalize how reading enhances life.	◆ Clear *consequences* for off-task behavior. Continuous dialogues about our literate lives.
◆ Students will make a plan of action at the start of each workshop. They will work their hardest to accomplish this goal.	◆ A format or way to record the *plan* for the day, and a routine for checking to see that plans have been completed.

SAMPLE READING WORKSHOP RULES FOR STUDENTS

1. I will listen carefully during the workshop mini-lesson.

- ◆ I will not chat with my friends at this time.
- ◆ I will raise my hand to answer or ask a question or to share a thought.

2. During quiet reading time I will read quietly.

- ◆ I will will read my book quietly.
- ◆ I will may talk about my book in a whisper voice to another student.
- ◆ I will may not talk about anything else besides the book.

3. I will not disturb anyone else who is quietly reading or writing.

4. I will remember to complete all of my jobs, such as recording on my log sheet and writing in my journal.

5. I will follow all directions when they are given.

6. I will read, read, read, and think, think, think.

Once you have established a set of rules that you believe are fair but to the point, it's time to think about enforcing these rules. Remember that how you handle the bumps in the road contributes greatly to the overall atmosphere of the Workshop. There is a fine line between helping students to realize their potential for doing the right thing and forcing them to read a book against their will. Reading should never be connected with punishment. The moment you say to a child, "You need to start reading, or I will take such and such away from you," you have turned that reader off for at least the day, if not for a longer period of time. Although a teacher can really never plan for disruption, it pays to be proactive by thinking through a few potential road bumps:

- 📖 Make plans for modeling, discussing, and pointing out appropriate behaviors.

- 📖 Discuss with your students how these appropriate behaviors help to create better readers and more exciting interactions with books.

- 📖 Plan to work one-on-one with those three or four students who are going to have difficulties with the expectations.

- 📖 Plan how you will respond to those unavoidable moments when something has gone wrong. Know what you're going to do beforehand, instead of trying to solve the problem when you're annoyed that someone made a bad choice and is taking up the class's precious reading time.

Scheduling the Time

Creating a schedule involves referring to the basic structure of a Reading Workshop and assigning a time limit for each component. Take a look at the sample schedules on page 22. Notice that they all are organized basically the same way. However, a few adjustments were made to accommodate students' ability levels, time constraints, and teacher preference—all of which play an important role in scheduling the Workshop.

A READING WORKSHOP SCHEDULE

...adapted for a second-grade classroom

9:30–9:40	Whole class daily edit or grammar review and re-teach
9:40–9:50	Daily read aloud, teacher think aloud
9:50–10:00	Planned Workshop mini-lesson and read aloud discussion
10:00–10:35	Independent reading; guided reading lessons, small skill groups, individual reading conferences, student response to texts
10:35–10:50	Reading journal; response to independent reading
10:50–11:00	Whole class meeting: journal share time, book talks, and Workshop wrap-up

A READING WORKSHOP SCHEDULE

...adapted for a fourth-grade classroom

9:30–9:40	Whole class daily edit or grammar review and re-teach
9:40–9:50	Daily read aloud, teacher think-aloud
9:50–10:00	Planned Workshop mini-lesson and read aloud discussion
10:00–10:50	"Me Time" for students' independent reading; small skill groups, individual reading conferences, student response to texts in small discussion groups or in personal reading journals
10:50–11:00	Whole-class meeting; journal share time, book talks and Workshop wrap-up

More than likely, your schedule will change a bit during the first few weeks of school. Real readers are not tied to the hands of a clock—most of us probably can't recall the last time we sat down with a book and said, "I will read for exactly 20 minutes and then I will stop." You may find you need just a few more minutes for the read aloud. Or perhaps you don't need quite as long to respond to the reading. Minor changes are inevitable.

Although flexibility is key to your Reading Workshop schedule, you don't want to send the message that you can extend reading time just on a whim. That would most likely result in many students taking their "good ol' time" getting started. Your decisions to end one component and flow into the next should reflect the idea that reading and writing are natural activities, and in the Workshop they do not need to end immediately as soon as the bell rings. As long as the overall structure and sequence of the Workshop remain consistent, students should manage well with the flexibility.

TEACHER to TEACHER

A schedule for a first-grade class may require a larger chunk of time for independent reading than one for an older class, because more first graders will need small, guided reading groups. First-grade teachers therefore should consider what could be offered as a break from quiet reading. Listening centers, word work centers, and pointers for reading around the room are all good examples of book nook breaks.

Planning Your Classroom Space

With your expectations in mind, your plan for managing student behavior and your schedule sketched in, you know what you are looking for in the Workshop model. You know, more

Revisiting the Reading Workshop: Management, Mini-Lessons, and Strategies • Scholastic Professional Books

specifically, what you want to see happening in your classroom. And you know, basically, what you want your actual classroom to look like. As you continue to create this vision, keep in mind the fact that there are some physical classroom requirements of a Reading Workshop. An effective Reading Workshop classroom has all or most of the following physical features:

- A meeting area—for mini-lessons, read alouds, and share time

- A substantial library that is central, exciting, and quite noticeable. Its presence in the room should help to create a certain ambiance that embraces literacy. Depending on your goals, you may need to design the library with space to house a book checkout system. (The next section offers detailed advice on how to accomplish all of this.)

- Comfortable places to read. Consider pillows, bean bag chairs, and carpet samples that students can move easily.

- An area where you can meet with small groups and still have a view of the other students in their book nooks

- Housing for teacher records

- Housing for student records and/or journals

- Housing of other reading materials such as sticky notes, bookmarks, and writing tools

- Places to hang charts, word walls, poems, and strategy reminders (preferably at students' eye level)

Set Up the Classroom Library

The classroom library center is where much of "the action" happens. Classroom libraries provide the substance that drives the independent reading portion of each Reading Workshop. As the focal point of the room, the library tells all who enter how you and your students feel about reading in general. It's also the place where kids make some pretty crucial decisions regarding their own literacy progress. Creating this magical place does take some time, determination, and patience.

Seek Out Sources for Books

Students in Reading Workshop classrooms read a lot. First graders who would typically read one or two small books in their guided reading group read 10 to 15 small books in the Reading Workshop. Fifth graders who would typically read and respond in a literature circle to one book every two weeks read 2 to 3 books each week.

One crucial job of teachers in the Reading Workshop involves making sure that students have all the books they need. Therefore, the first—and arguably most important—task in building your classroom library is to figure out how and from where you will obtain all the books you need. Here are some possible ways, means, and sources to consider:

- Look to your school's supply of trade books.

- Use what is already in your classroom library.

- Cash in your book club points.

- Keep your eyes open for sale tables at bookstores.

- Request parental donations. Some might be willing to sponsor a magazine subscription for your class.

- Investigate school business partner donations.

- Look into local mini-grants.

- Collect as many used books of any kind from as many places as you can think of. Trade in these books to a used bookstore and spend the profit on appropriate books for your library.

- Ask parents to send books for your class in lieu of holiday or end-of-school presents.

- Invite students to add their own collections to your library. (Be clear about the checkout procedure for borrowed books.)

- Talk to your school librarian. Find out if your students can have easy access to the library during your Workshop times.

- Contact textbook publishers. Some are able to donate trade books that accompany their texts after adoption procedures have been completed.

- Depending on the socio-economic status of your school district, you might be able begin a "Birthday Book" program where parents donate one book in honor of their child's birthday.

- Check out sales at your local public library. Bargains hide in funny places!

- Search and scour—don't be shy about your hunt for books. Having others keep their eyes out for you may result in even more books!

One final word of caution: As you follow up on all of these wonderful and economical leads, it's important to remember your commitment to good literature. There are lots of great buys out there. However, there are also a lot of books with prices that are greatly reduced for good reason. Trust your instincts!

Organize Your Literature Collection for Optimal Student Use

Just having the books in the library brings you about halfway toward achieving your goal that children will read often, select wisely, and experience a variety of genres. Now you need to create order on the shelves of your library. And again, organization is the key.

There are three main ways to group books: by level, by genre, or by a combination of the two. Teachers in the lower grades may want to focus solely on leveled categories. Upper-grade teachers may want to offer more variation by genre, yet still

A third-grade library provides easy access to books grouped mostly by genres.

provide leveled options for students who need them. The following diagrams and discussions illustrate the many possible ways to organize an effective Reading Workshop library.

Key Points in a First-Grade Classroom Library

Students in the early primary grades require eye-catching libraries. The library shelves of a first- or early second-grade class ought to pull the students into the library area with titles and characters they know and love. Little ones also might require some encouragement to try something new. In short, a primary library ought to be safe, warm, inviting, and accommodating.

Consider the following suggestions and the illustration at right to help you set up a first-grade classroom library:

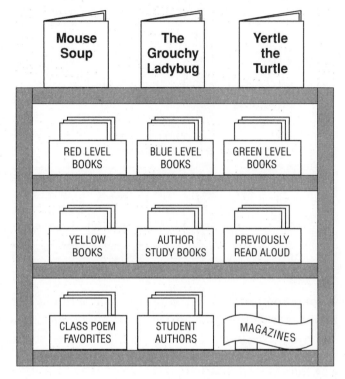

A SAMPLE FIRST-GRADE CLASSROOM LIBRARY

- 📖 Keep most books in leveled bins to aid students who are learning to make their own "just right" choices.

- 📖 Use colored stick-on dots to help ensure that students return books to the proper bins.

- 📖 Make available big books that already have been read aloud.

- 📖 Place multiple copies of individual books in some bins to encourage and support partner readings.

- 📖 If re-shelving becomes a problem in your room, take a tip from public libraries. Designate a bin or basket as the "Put me back!" place. Have one or two young "librarians" re-shelve them at the end of the day.

- 📖 House non-fiction books in science and social studies learning centers for students to read during independent reading time.

- 📖 Use a listening center for less independent readers.

- 📖 Place extra baskets of books on student tables/desks.

- 📖 Assign each child his or her own leveled box. It's more work for the teacher, but fewer book-choosing dilemmas occur for the students.

TEACHER to TEACHER

In our first-grade classroom, we have a bin of books we refer to as our "old friends." These books have been shared over and over with the students and are clearly their favorites. "Old friend" reading is an excellent way to practice one-to-one matching, concepts about print, and story structure. We require each first grader to enjoy at least two "old friends" every day during independent reading.

Key Points in a Primary-Grade Classroom Library

A Sample Second-Grade (mid-year) Classroom Library

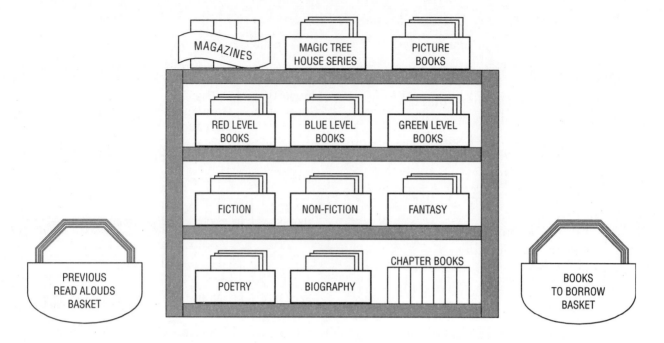

Second and third graders know their way around library shelves. Most know which types of books they like to read, and most are able to decide which book is just right for them. The library shelves in these classrooms must be well stocked and well organized. Students should be able to locate what it is they are looking for, and they should be intrigued to try something new as they peruse the shelves. In setting up a primary-level library, try to balance beloved characters and series with new, interesting, and age-appropriate titles.

Consider the following suggestions and the illustration above to help you set up a primary-level classroom library:

- At mid year, most students are well able to select their own "just right" book from a genre bin. (Color coding for level with sticker dots is still helpful and worth the time it takes to mark each book.) However, for those students who remain skittish about making a good choice, maintain a few leveled bins to select from.

- Make social studies and science content books available to students. (However, you may need to change the checkout procedures for these types of books since many might be from the public library.)

- In the borrowed book basket, keep books from students' own personal collections that they wanted to share. Have separate rules and checkout guidelines for these books.

- Continue to encourage less independent readers to use the listening center.

- In addition to grouping by genre, group books by series. Students often get hooked on a particular author or series; grouping favorite books this way helps to keep up the momentum between books.

- After a book has been read aloud, it is more accessible to students in independent reading. House read alouds together to tell even struggling readers that, "Hey, you know this book. You have a great shot at reading it successfully!"

Key Points in an Intermediate Classroom Library
A Sample Intermediate Classroom Library

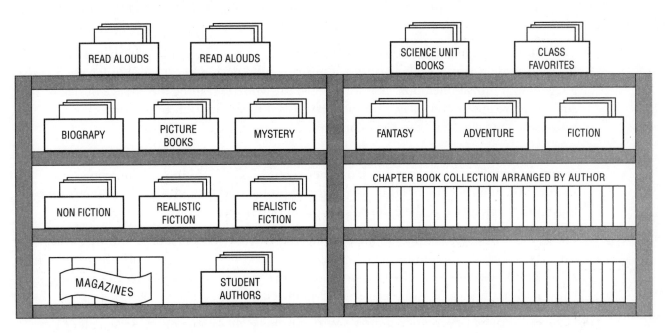

Students in the upper grades require a well-stocked classroom library. They need lots of choices within all genres. A well-stocked intermediate library offers students the chance to practice book selection skills they will continue to use as adult readers in libraries and book stores. Frequent browsing in the classroom library helps students to choose books more quickly and carefully, allowing for strong momentum between books.

Consider the following suggestions and the illustration above to help you set up an intermediate-level classroom library:

- Organization and grouping of books should always reflect the particular class's needs, abilities, and tastes. For example, this class library reflects a class with diverse tastes. Another class, which may have many students who love to read mysteries, might have separate bins for "Boxcar Children" books and for "Enclyclopedia Brown" books.

- Your decision regarding whether or not to color code for levels will depend on the abilities of the students in your room. It will be more important in third grade than it will be in fifth grade.

- Make picture books available to all readers.

- Place some chapter books on the shelves with the spine out. This helps to accquaint students with the book-choosing skills they will need at public libraries and at book stores.

Establish a Book Checkout System

Having the library area of your room set up and ready for your Reading Workshop is a wonderful experience. Because you are able to step back and literally see the effects of the hard work you put in, it may also be one of the most satisfying processes in your preparation to transform your classroom.

However, as soon as you sit back and admire all of your hard work, you realize that, very soon, little fingers will begin to rummage through your shelves, mixing up your grand design.

Luckily, though, you'll be prepared—you'll have anticipated their energy. Your students' excitement to read and their lack of attention to detail is precisely the reason you'll need some type of book checkout system. Here are a few variations on the same "bring your book back" theme:

- Have students sign out the book they are reading. A large *"Sign Out" binder* with a section for each student works well. This idea is mostly useful with upper-grade students who take a few days to finish one book. Beginning readers, who are reading an average of five to six small picture books every day, should not be asked to record each title for checkout purposes. That would be too time-consuming.

- Depending on your organizational ability, you might be able to rely on your students' *individual reading logs* to keep track of where your books are hiding. If you choose to monitor the library contents this way, you will probably want to house all of the reading logs in the same place at the end of the Workshop session.

- Have students write their names on a *clothespin*. As students take a book out of a bin, they can attach their clothespin to the rim of the bin. Because this system works best if you have all of your books organized by level and you know exactly what books are in each bin, it lends itself more to a first- or early second-grade classroom.

- Have each student decorate a *library pocket* with his or her name on it. Attach all of the cards to a "Library Checkout" bulletin board or pocket chart. (See the photo below for an illustration.) Take the time to write the title of each book on an index card and place the card in the book like a bookmark (or in a library pocket in each book). As students take books from the library, they can place the title card in the pocket with their name on it. When they return the book, they put the title card back in the book before re-shelving it. As far as prep work goes, this idea is the most time-consuming at first. But it also is the most foolproof system we've seen. And it's effective no matter what grade level you are working with.

- A variation on the library pocket system at right, which works better for older students, is to assign each student a pocket (or page in a notebook or binder, etc). The student records the title of the book he or she has checked out of the classroom library. When the student returns the book, he can check it off his list.

While requiring a good deal of preparation, library pockets are a very effective part of a checkout system.

It's important to share with your students how much hard work you put into creating the classroom library. Don't be afraid to spend lots of time in the beginning of the year discussing, modeling, and praising appropriate library upkeep. Know that the time you spend monitoring how students use the library is time well spent. Discuss with students the "hows" and "whys" of managing your great library. Try to lead them to realize how important and special it is, and soon they will become its best, and most careful, librarians.

Limit Number of Books

A classroom library can house only a certain number of books. It's wise, then, to limit the number of books that students can check out of your library. This proves more important in the early grades, when students are reading numerous titles each day. If students are able to take only one book at a time, some might spend more time getting up and finding another book than they do actually reading. On the other hand, you don't want students taking ten to twelve books back to their book nook with them. If you are going to allow multiple checkouts, you probably need a safe means of transport for all those books. For instance, provide young readers with a small gift bag, create reading baskets, or purchase a supply of magazine file boxes for your students to use. Then allow some time for students to "go shopping" for three to five books. Students can take their shopping bags or book boxes full of books to their nooks and remain there until reading time is over.

Use Book Boxes During Independent Reading Times

Our primary students use cardboard book boxes to house the books that they are reading. These book boxes are 9 x 12 x 4 inch file boxes. Each student has his own box with his name on the front. Students get their book boxes at the beginning of the reading time, take the book boxes right to their book nooks, and read without interruption for the duration of the independent reading time. In addition to storing the students' reading books, these boxes can hold the reading journal, reading log, bookmarks, or sticky notes. Having the book box readily available cuts down on time spent looking for books and leaves more time for reading.

Books can be placed into the book boxes in a number of ways:

- The reading specialist helps the students make book choices.

- The classroom teacher adds books she knows are appropriate for the student.

- The student adds books from home, the classroom library, or the school library.

- The classroom teacher adds books that were read by the student during a guided reading group.

- The students swap books with other students.

Invite Students and Parents into the Workshop "Community"

With the classroom set up, the library shelves stocked, and details about rules and scheduling up and running, you are ready to open the doors to those people who matter most: your students and their parents. We return again and again in our discussions to the notion that a Reading Workshop classroom operates as a community. A sense of "we're all in this together" often emerges during our literature discussions and our share time.

At this point, you can shift your role from being the person in charge to being one of the people in charge of the Workshop. By giving students choices and responsibility, and by keeping parents informed, you let the other stakeholders into the organization and management of the Reading Workshop.

Provide Book Nooks for Independent Reading Time

Aside from enjoying the morning paper with a cup of tea, neither one of us regularly reads at the kitchen table. As adults, we find it hard to settle in to a story if we're uncomfortable. Book nooks are based on the idea that student readers work the same way. In their own, comfy places to read, students are more able to settle into the story; they are able to act like real readers.

Book nooks are, very simply, places around the room where students may read. Book nooks can be as simple as carpet squares. They might be more elaborate, such as chairs, couches, or beanbag chairs. Or they can be designated spots around the room, such as next to a filing cabinet, in front of a window, or under a table.

Look around your room and decide where book nooks might be and where they should not be. When your students arrive, take a field trip around the room and talk about all the places that they might want to "claim" as their own. Give the kids a week or so to try out a couple of places. Then draw a map of the room showing the location of each student's nook to create a type of book nook seating chart. If you're lucky enough to have more desirable places like window seats or special furniture, work out a rotating system. For example, in a room with two beanbag chairs, you might assign one to the week's line leader and one to the week's door holder. Or in a room with more furniture options, assign each student a number, and post which number gets which piece of furniture that week.

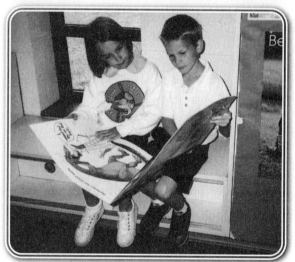

Finally, it's important to note that book nooks are a Reading Workshop privilege, not a right. Students who have difficulty focusing in their nooks often shape up when back in their own desks. It's essential to work out ahead of time what the rules are and an overall system for book nook use.

Book nooks allow students of all ages a chance to get comfortable as they settle in with a good story.

Organize Records and Reading Materials

Although knowing where you'll keep your students' records is a minor detail when compared to all of the other Workshop goals, it's nonetheless one you should tackle before students enter the picture. Consider possible locations for the following things:

- 📖 Student reading journals and/or student reading folders
- 📖 Class set of book boxes or reading bags
- 📖 Teacher files of students' progress
- 📖 Binders, hanging files, or large notebooks containing assessment results of individual students

It also helps to determine a centrally-located place to store supplies that students may need during independent time, including:

- 📖 Sticky notes
- 📖 Sharpened pencils (There's nothing worse than a pencil sharpener grind in the midst of a quiet reading room.)
- 📖 Bookmarks
- 📖 Highlighter

Create a Reading Workshop Companion Book

Creating a "Companion Book" for intermediate students to use during reading time is helpful. Binding the required Workshop forms into a book helps to reduce the cluttered reading folders that often only add to the task of keeping things neat and orderly. Instead of trying to handle a loose collection of reading logs, main idea notes, required reading records, etc., students are able to keep everything together.

We issue a Companion Book to students every quarter. At the start of the marking period, we decide what the students will need for that period: for example, the number of reading log sheets and the amount of mini-lesson notes. All of the pages are bound (either with plastic binding combs or just stapled) and the students wind up with a booklet that keeps all their reading pages together in one place. Here is a sample list of what might be included in a Companion Book. The items with an asterisk are included in this chapter.

- 📖 Reading Record Sheets* (page 35)
- 📖 Mini-Lesson Main Idea! notes* (above)
- 📖 Reading Workshop rules
- 📖 Required genre reading pages for that quarter
- 📖 Response pages used for assessment (Prove it! Page)* (at right)
- 📖 Reading conference notes page
- 📖 Independent Reading Guide* (page 36)

Name _____ Week of _____

Mini-Lesson Main Idea!

Monday: _____

Tuesday: _____

Wednesday: _____

Thursday: _____

Friday: _____

My favorite read aloud story this week was _____ because _____

Name _____ Week of _____

Prove it! Page

Review your mini-lesson notes from the last two weeks. Tell about 2 of the lessons in your own words. Don't forget the main idea!

1. _____

2. _____

Review your reading journal and reading log from the last two weeks. Choose one reading you have done and write a strong journal entry about that reading.

Write one final reaction to something you have accomplished during the last two weeks in our Reading Workshop. (What would you like me to know?)

📖 Reference pages (Points to remember when responding, How to select a just right book, What to do when you're stuck on a word, etc.)

Depending on your own needs, you may even use the Companion Book for assessment or for support during parent conferences at the end of the marking period. You may want to hang on to all the Companion Books until the end of the year to help the children celebrate all of their successes of the year.

Keep Parents Informed

The one component that may be easy to overlook as you set up a Reading Workshop classroom may in fact be one of the most important. You will need to inform the students' parents about the changes.

Your students' parents probably did not learn to read in book nooks. Often, it's hard for parents to support that which they do not understand, and rightly so. It becomes, then, your job to help parents understand why increased independent reading time and time for meaningful reflection are such powerful and essential elements of a strong reading program. It has worked for us to discuss the Workshop at our Back-to-School and Open House nights in September. We distribute small packets of Reading Workshop information that parents can take away with them.

Whatever your own approach, be sure to encourage an open dialogue. Parents will be on board with the program as soon as they see great things happening. It's just a lot easier to get a head start by telling them what to look for. The following list describes a few ways we have been able to "let parents in on" the secrets of our Reading Workshops:

📖 Invite parents to visit and/or volunteer during Reading Workshop time.

📖 Share the schedule, rationale, and expectations with them at the very start of the year.

📖 Send a weekly newsletter home that contains the week's mini-lessons and read-aloud titles and other similar books that they can check out of the local library.

📖 Train parents to become reading coaches at home. Share some secrets of good reading conferences that focus on strategic reading.

📖 Ask all parents to write down any questions they have about the Reading Workshop periodically throughout the year. Compile all of the questions and your responses in one newsletter to go out to all parents.

📖 Have a colleague videotape you and your students during one Reading Workshop. Allow parents to check out the video and a pamphlet that explains what they are seeing.

📖 Create a parent information packet to distribute at the beginning of the year and to new students as they arrive. Information we have shared in such packets includes a copy of the Reading Workshop schedule, a letter to the parents (see page 33), and suggested ways to help at home.

One final word: As with anything new, challenges will arise as you set up a Reading Workshop. It's the solutions to the problems that are always surprising us. Many times, it's the kids themselves who create solutions to small snags in the Workshop. We have held many mini-lessons entirely devoted to ironing out the kinks of a mid-year Workshop. Things happen. Teachers and students respond together, helping to make our community of readers stronger each day. We've enjoyed watching our young readers succeed by holding firmly to our belief of "Whatever works, just keep 'em reading!"

Dear Parents,

Your child is already enjoying a wonderful reading and writing experience in first grade. Through our Reading Workshop, your child's language arts program provides opportunities to participate in reading as "real readers" do. It also allows us the opportunity to tailor instruction more individually and appropriately for each student in the class. In this way, more time is available for children to read. Research suggests that the amount of independent reading time children do in school is related to gains in reading achievement. Independent reading is also a major source of vocabulary growth and reading fluency.

However, we do not mean to suggest that students are left on their own to "just read." A balanced reading program with quality instruction involves many elements. In the Reading Workshop, students have an opportunity to:

- listen to and respond to good literature.
- participate in individual and small-group reading instruction and read individually and/or with other children.
- select material at the appropriate level.
- have lessons on phonics and word attack skills.
- participate in lessons on using many reading strategies.
- focus on comprehension.
- integrate reading and writing activities.

A Reading Workshop gives students an opportunity to communicate with their teacher as well as with other students—both orally and in writing. Students have opportunities to make choices about what they are interested in reading. They are also provided guidance in choosing from various types of literature—realistic fiction, nonfiction, poetry, etc. All of these experiences incorporate our local curriculum's standards as well as the state's standards.

We believe that the ultimate goal in reading is personal understanding and enjoyment. Within our Reading Workshop, we watch our students display these characteristics every day. They are truly motivated to read, and to read well.

We appreciate your continued involvement in your child's reading and invite you to come in and read with us.

Happy Reading,

Marybeth Alley
Classroom teacher

Barbara Orehovec
Reading Specialist

Help at home...

You can strengthen the Reading Workshop activities as you read with your child every night!

- Be sure to read every night. One book, two books, more than that! You decide. Practice is absolutely necessary! Depending on the book your child is reading, s/he may read to you, or you could take turns reading aloud with your child.

- When reading with your child at home, here are some pointers to keep in mind:

  - Begin books by looking closely at them. Notice the cover illustrations, the author, and the illustrator. Are there any clues as to what the book will be about? Does the back of the book have any information to give the reader? Take a picture walk through SOME of the pages. Discuss what you both think might happen in the book.

  - Stop every once and a while to ask your child to retell the story. He or she should have a picture of it in his/her mind. If it's not clear that your child is understanding the story, backtrack and talk more together as the story unfolds.

  - Stop every so often and ask your child to predict what might happen next. Make sure he has a reason for his thinking. (Not just, "I think Goldilocks will like the little bed." But, "I think Goldilocks will like the Little Bear's bed because she is little too, and she liked his porridge and his little chair."

  - Encourage your child to ask questions while you read.

  - After reading a story or chapter, stop and have a conversation about the book. What did you like/dislike? Did it remind you of another book or a time in your life? Why do you think the characters acted the way that they did? And so on.

- When your child stumbles (or stops) at an unknown word, it's best to not just tell what the word is or to say simply, "Sound it out." Try using the following prompts instead:

  - Get your mouth ready to say that word.

  - Does that word look like any other word that you do know?

  - Is there a chunk of the word that you do know?

  - What word would make sense there?

  - Do the letters match?

- Have fun and be a model. Show your child that reading is important to you and your lifestyle. Talk, talk, talk, and listen, listen, listen about books and life. Oral language adds immensely to your child's vocabulary and fluency development.

Name _____

Date _____

Reading Record Sheet for _____

Date	Type	Title	Pages	Genre

TYPES: RA = Read Aloud book   JR = Just Right Book   E = Easy Book   H = Hard Book

Independent Reading Guide

Today I am reading _____

I think I will find something out about _____

_____

Before I begin to read, here are two things I wonder about:

_____

_____

During my reading, I will notice my thinking. When I notice that I am "thinking above the text," I will write what I am thinking on a sticky note. When I'm done reading, I will place all the sticky notes here.

_____

_____

_____

_____

_____

_____

_____

My reading today was mostly about

_____

_____

After reading today, I now know

_____

_____

Revisiting the Reading Workshop: Management, Mini-Lessons, and Strategies • Scholastic Professional Books

CHAPTER 3

PREPARING TO TEACH:

How to Plan for and Structure Successful Mini-Lessons

"Once I completed the long-term planning, I was able to see the 'big picture,' and day-to-day planning became less of a challenge."

— Mrs. Rachael Persinger (4th grade teacher)

Mini-lessons provide teachers with the forum to share information, to teach reading strategies, and to help students appreciate literature as they become independent readers.

The mini-lesson is a key component of the Reading Workshop, because it starts the Workshop and provides a focus for the day. This is the time when you and the readers in your class come together as a community. It is the portion of the Reading Workshop where you engage in planned direct teaching—sharing information, knowledge, and tools in order to help your young readers grow. Here the teacher can "let students in on" the secrets about reading strategies and skills that great readers know and use throughout their lives.

Because they play such a pivotal instructional role in the Workshop, mini-lessons require real planning. Like all good lesson plans, mini-lessons are built upon student needs, incorporating guidelines from local and state curricula as well as the teacher's knowledge of students strengths and weaknesses. Mini-lessons also require structure. The teacher and the student each have a distinct and active role to play. The smoothest mini-lessons evolve when thought has been given to everything from instructional details to transitions into and out of lesson time. This chapter focuses on both planning and structuring mini-lessons so that you can make the most of them for your students.

We begin our mini-lessons in the same way each day. We invite our students to "the carpet" (our meeting area). We all sit together, close yet comfortable, and begin to talk about our reading lives—what we've done the previous day and where we are headed that particular day. By gathering together at the meeting area, we are saying to our students, "Our reading community is coming together again. Come on in. Get comfortable. You can certainly expect a great story to delight you and some good conversation to inspire you. Ready?"

> ## TEACHER to TEACHER
>
> We realize that there are such things as limited classroom space and bigger bodies in the fourth and fifth grade. But we feel it's necessary to create some area in your room where you can gather even in these older classes. Perhaps some students can sit in chairs and some on the floor. Reading aloud and discussing great books is a magical part of every Reading Workshop. We urge you to set it apart from the routine of sitting in desks, chairs, groups, and rows. As adults, we do not read or discuss that way. We should not be asking our students to do so either.

Planning Mini-Lessons

There are several types of mini-lessons (Atwell 1988; Hindley 1996):

📖 Procedures and management

📖 Reading process (strategies and skills)

📖 Literary elements and literary techniques (author's craft)

In subsequent chapters, we describe each type of mini-lesson, suggest possible topics, provide you with a list of literature to use, and show you examples of each type of mini-lesson. For now though, take a look at the following planning tool that will give you assistance in planning your mini-lessons.

THINKING THROUGH THE READING WORKSHOP MINI-LESSON

In planning the mini-lesson for a Reading Workshop, strive to follow these steps for your lesson.

1. Begin with a *connection* to and/or review previous lessons and strategies. Use a conversational format that avoids numerous leading questions. See what students know and can talk about.

2. Provide a *rationale* for the lesson's topic. Why should students want to add it to their reading repertoire?

3. Incorporate a *read aloud* to further extend the main topic of the mini-lesson. Talk with students before, during, and after the story, emphasizing how the story can help them think about the main idea of the mini-lesson.

4. Help students *set a purpose* for listening to the companion read aloud story. Share (or hint at) the connection between the lesson topic and the read aloud.

5. *Revisit* the main lesson topic after completing the read aloud. Ask students to use their own words to discuss the new idea.

6. Encourage students to *apply* what was learned in their own independent reading that day. Ask students, "When you are in your book nook today, how can you use what we have just talked about in our mini-lesson?"

A Recommended Planning Form

The planning form on the next page is a useful tool that can help you anticipate and balance out the key elements of your mini-lessons. We encourage teachers who are new to planning mini-lessons to use forms such as this because they help in building consistency among mini-lessons. The forms may become unnecessary as you continue to plan and deliver similar mini-lessons, but at first they are an invaluable support. Although the forms may seem to require a lot of information, they provide a great way to get you thinking about what goes into a successful lesson.

The first form, page 40, is a template version with simple directions on how to use the form. The second form, page 41, is a completed lesson plan for a procedural mini-lesson on the student's role in conferencing; it demonstrates a vital lesson in the first weeks of your Reading Workshop.

Long-term and Short-term Planning

We've heard many reading teachers remark on how easy planning for the day's lesson is once some long-term planning has taken place. Long-term planning consists of a listing of all the major topics and subtopics you plan on covering with your students during the course of your year together. It's a good idea to start with the objectives you are required to teach in your area and then to add topics to tailor instruction for your own grade level and student needs. The strategies and skills listed throughout this book also provide a great starting point for your own long-term planning.

Once you have a working document of mini-lesson topics, weekly planning for the mini-lesson is fairly simple: with your students' needs and your district's objectives in mind, glance over the topic chart and select the topics for the week. We find it extremely helpful to record when the lesson was taught and what read aloud book was used to teach the lesson. Then it's very easy to see where we've been, where we need to go, and where we need to go back to each time we plan a mini-lesson.

Planning for the short term—perhaps a week—involves selecting the mini-lesson topic or topics, matching and gathering read alouds that correspond to the topic, pre-reading the read alouds yourself, making a plan for the direct instruction, and planning for any small groups you might hold. You cannot plan for individual conferences or any small groups you may spontaneously call. In essence, then, for a Reading Workshop that could last over an hour, you are planning mainly for the mini-lesson that should last around twenty minutes. And that is not a bad deal!

Depending on the topics you have selected for the week, you may wish to create some sort of theme or unit of study. On the top of page 42 is an example of a weekly plan for a second-grade class. During this week, the teacher incorporated time for review, discussion and exploration of a new genre, and an author study. Her flexible small group even worked with poems that fit into the *Strega Nona* theme.

> **TEACHER to TEACHER**
> When sitting down to do your weekly plans, think about planning for Monday through Thursday only. Save Friday's mini-lesson to address specific needs that come up during the week's other mini-lessons or during reading conferences. For example, a fifth-grade class has been discussing imagery all week. However, from her work in individual conferences, the teacher notices that many of her students would benefit from a discussion about prefixes and suffixes. On Friday, she'll do a mini-lesson on the topic for all of her students.

READING STRATEGY MINI-LESSON LESSON PLAN: _____

(TOPIC)

Rationale—

◆ Explain why you are teaching this particular lesson.

◆ What are students doing as readers, and what are you going to teach to help them be better readers?

Literature—Choose appropriate literature.

Materials—Share materials to spark interest.

Connection—Make a connection and/or review previous lessons/strategies.

Purpose—

◆ Set a purpose for listening to the lesson/story.

◆ Connect the topic to the read aloud.

Instruction—

◆ Provide instruction for before, during, and after reading.

◆ Extend the main topic throughout the reading.

◆ Stop as appropriate and think aloud, demonstrate, provide instruction.

◆ Before sending students off to independent reading, charge them with the task of applying the mini-lesson in their reading.

Questions for Discussion—

◆ Revisit the topic.

◆ Involve students in discussion.

Related Conference or Journal Focus—Apply new learning to independent reading and response.

Additional Literature to Use for Strategy Reinforcement—Additional literature suggestions.

READING STRATEGY MINI-LESSON LESSON PLAN: STUDENT'S ROLE IN A READING CONFERENCE

Rationale—Students need to know what is expected of them in a conference.

Materials—Show clipboard, notebook, or whatever you use for taking notes. Also share whatever materials you will bring to a conference (sticky notes, bookmarks, magnetic letters, dry erase board).

Connection—"Yesterday we talked about what my job is in a conference. Today we will focus on your job."

Purpose—"It is really important that you listen closely today. I am going to let you know what I expect of you when I come and meet with you for a reading conference."

Instruction—

◆ "Today when I come to your book nook for a conference, I want you to just continue doing what you are doing—whether you are in the middle of reading or if you are doing a written response. If you are reading with a partner or in a small group, that's okay, too. I will just listen in a little bit first.

◆ If I ask you to read to me, just continue where you are. I will be taking some notes as you do this.

◆ I might ask you to tell me what is going on in your story. If it is fiction, I will expect to hear about the characters, where the story takes place, what is happening. If it is nonfiction, I will expect to hear about what you are learning.

◆ I will probably then do a little teaching—just for you. Your job is to listen to what I'm teaching and then try what I ask. Do you have any questions?"

Questions for Discussion—

◆ "Why do you think I just want to watch you read for a minute or so?"

◆ "Why will I be taking notes?"

◆ "How should my teaching help you?"

◆ "What will I expect you to be able to do after I teach you a little lesson?"

Related Conference or Journal Focus—

◆ "Today in your reading I want you to think about what we tried together. Try that on your own."

◆ "Today as you write, think about our conference. Write how you applied that today."

More often than not, though, the week's planning does not gel together as nicely as this. In the planning example below, the teacher focused on the strategy of questioning throughout the entire week. Here, instead of choosing read alouds that connect to one another, the teacher purposely chose read alouds that differ greatly. In this way, she was able to show her students that readers use reading strategies all the time, regardless of what type of book they are reading. This should help her

Weekly Workshop Planning

	Monday	Tuesday	Wednesday	Thursday	Friday
Read Aloud	Strega Nona HerStory (dePaola)	Strega Nona dePaola	Big Anthony & the Magic King dePaola	The Art Lesson dePaola	The Magic Lesson dePaola
Mini-Lesson Focus	Story elements review -setting purpose for rdg Shared Reading-Magic Pasta Pat Words	New genre study FANTASY Discuss how story is a fantasy, charact-istics of genre Shared Rdg	Context clues to determine meanings of the unknown Italian words Review fantasy	Compare and Contrast Fantasy & Reality	Retelling story in Proper Sequence
Independent Reading Group	ay, ack, ant, ar chunking word sorts	ate, air, all ake chunking word sorts	Context Clues through Big Book reading	Guided Rdg group of Fluffy	Hands-on sequencing lesson w/ story cards
Flexible Small Group	Spaghetti Poem introduction & Shared rdg.	Poem shared rdg & discussion	Poem intro & shared reading	Poem shared reading & discussion	/
Journal & Share Focus	Purpose for reading your book today? or other opinions	Are you reading a fantasy? How can you tell? What genre are you reading? How do you know?	Unprompted	Venn diagram to compare book you are reading now with another book	retell story read today in proper sequence Then give your opinion about the book

WEEKLY WORKSHOP PLANNING

	Read Aloud	Mini-Lesson Focus	Small Reading Level-Based Group	Small Skill-Based Group
Monday	The Raft	Review/reteach story elements including movement through time and change	Guided Reading all week

Little Kid | Decoding multi-syllabic words in context—students to begin list of new, big words in reading journal |
Tuesday	Knots on a Counting Rope	Introduction to questioning strategy—good readers ask questions as they read	My Monster Friends	Fluency group—poetry share "The Pet Store"
Wednesday	Cactus Hotel	Questioning—finding answers within the text	Odd Socks	None planned—hold extra conferences. Check in with story chat group
Thursday	Be Good to Eddie Lee	Questioning a character's motives	Ratty-Tatty	Meet again with Monday's group for review/reteach/assessment
Friday	The Wednesday Surprise	Using inferences to answer questions about the plot	What's Around the Corner?	None planned—sit in on story chat

students make the leap to applying the strategy in books they will read in their book nooks.

As you look at these plans, you may be surprised to find only two groups included on each. Remember that because so much instruction is given to individuals during reading conferences, it is rare that you will hold more than two groups during one day's Workshop. The other students' needs are being met individually. Note also that the second group is skill based and therefore will include different students each day.

Good Plans Lead to Expected and Unexpected Instruction

When you start planning mini-lessons, you may think you are going to concentrate on a specific skill or strategy that day, such as "making inferences." However, you'll probably come to realize that one read aloud lends itself to many potential lessons. For example, as you lead your students through a read aloud on making inferences, you discover that you are also:

- drawing on background knowledge.

- making connections with another text.

- re-reading to clarify meaning.

- questioning.

- visualizing.

- drawing conclusions.

After all, good readers do all of these things while reading. They do not rely on just one strategy at a time. Initially, try to keep your mini-lessons focused on one idea. But chances are it won't take long before you'll become comfortable enough to expand your mini-lesson discussions.

What's magical about the potential of the "expandable" mini-lesson is the amount of reading instruction your students can actually receive. The teacher may be reading *Knots on a Counting Rope* to illustrate the use of the questioning strategy, but the students might lead her to a quick review of a "story within a story" story pattern or of a different text format. We review many lessons, skills, and strategies every day for the simple reason that we share good literature every day. Good reading instruction is good reading instruction. Good literature is good literature. And, with guidance, your students are bound to make the connections.

At right are some other pointers to keep in mind as you plan for the week.

PLANNING POINTERS

- The read aloud is very important. All good lessons have a hook, and the read aloud is it for the mini-lesson. Try not to pass up this opportunity.

- There are times when a mini-lesson topic does not mesh perfectly with a read aloud book. Don't be afraid to get a little creative with the connection.

- It's fine to use a good book for more than one lesson. All mature readers reread favorite books. Think of this as just one more chance to help students experience the many layers of good literature.

- Never be afraid to let go of the topic you had in mind if the students present a true need or desire to go in a different direction. Remember, your job is to teach your students to love reading and to help them discover the joys of reading. You are not there simply to "cover topics" through the mini-lesson forum. You can always go back to your planned topic the next day.

- Don't worry. You will get it all taught, and taught well. Having finished the required curriculum long before the year's end, many Reading Workshop teachers at all grade levels in our building search high and low in the last couple of weeks for mini-lesson topics. What a great opportunity for review and enrichment.

Structuring the Mini-Lesson

Mini-lessons require structure in order to be successful. This section looks at several different angles of structuring: the role of direct instruction, the students' particular responsibilities, and the transition routines that help close the lesson smoothly. Reflecting on each of these elements ahead of time should help you as you map out and begin your Reading Workshop.

Teacher-Directed Instruction

The read aloud and mini-lesson portion is by all means the most teacher-directed part of the Reading Workshop. This is the part of the Workshop that appears more traditional, with the teacher in the front of the room, showing and telling students about the reading process. The teacher, responsible for planning out the entire structure of the mini-lesson, often does the majority of the talking, while the students follow her lead throughout the lesson.

However, there is more here than meets the eye. During the mini-lesson instruction, the teacher maintains a dialogue with the students. This constant back and forth between teacher and students allows for ongoing assessment of where students are in their understanding. These conversations before, during, and after the story become the substance of the students' reading instruction. For instance, when students seem a bit timid about a new concept or strategy, you can return to passages and re-read them. You can model again, think out loud again, and continue to invite them to share in your experience. You do whatever you can to bring them in—in to understanding the story or the concept, in to the mind and processes of a competent reader, in to a community of readers. Teachers do more than teach about reading, they show students how it's done.

Student Responsibility During Mini-Lessons

In a good mini-lesson, the teacher may be leading, but the students do not remain passive. Fortunately, good literature makes the challenging task of teaching and simultaneously involving students a great deal easier. Choosing an enthralling read aloud helps ensure that your students will be on track with you throughout the lesson. When their interest is piqued, they will be eager to make connections between the topic of the mini-lesson and the book you have chosen to read to them. While your job is to keep bringing the students into the world of strategies, craft, and enjoyment, their job is to prove to you—primarily through focused questions and comments—that they are "getting it," making connections, and merging new information with what they already know.

Ideas for Involving Students

Following is a list of possible activities that may help you "bring students in" to your goal for the day. We've used these activities with success in all grades and with all levels of students. We like these particular activities because they involve all students, but do not force our more reserved students to feel like they have been "put on the spot."

Story Partners—Before beginning the read aloud, have one child in the circle touch the knee of the nearest student to the right. Those two students are "story partners" for the lesson. Proceed around the circle in this manner until all students have partners. During the read aloud, ask a question or offer a thought-provoking statement to the students. Story partners turn to each other to make their predictions, answer or ask questions, or comment in some other way. You can then get up from your chair and circulate among the conferring partners.

The idea is to quickly figure out what most students are thinking; this will inform you about how to proceed with the lesson. When you return to your seat, you might simply say something like, "Partners, look up," and make a comment about how most of the class is feeling or what you noticed about their observations. Then you can go on with the book. As you know, kids love to share. This activity allows everyone to talk, yet is also quite time efficient!

Story partners can talk together during the read aloud and mini-lesson and later during share time.

Thumbs up, Thumbs down, Listen and Find—In this activity, you tell students what they are listening for before the story begins. For example, during a reading of the book *Thunder Cake* by Patricia Polacco, you might tell students to give a "thumbs-up" when they are making a connection between the book and another book the class has read before. You then stop reading when you notice a number of students with their thumbs up. Try to predict why their thumbs are up and say something like, "I'll bet that this part about her grandmother is reminding you of the grandmother from *Some Birthday*. Or perhaps you are thinking of your own grandmother." If you've guessed their thought correctly, students will keep their thumbs up. If you haven't hit it on the nose, students will show a "thumbs-down" sign. Then make a quick decision. If there's time, ask for clarifications. If you'd rather keep the story moving at that point, say something like, "Wow, you're all making such strong connections about so many different things. That's what good readers do all the time. They think about what the book is reminding them of. Everybody put thumbs away and let's go on with the story."

TEACHER to TEACHER

In some cases, and in some classrooms, it is helpful to pre-plan who will be partners with whom (considering the needs, levels, and abilities of all students). When you have taken the time to plan out partners, it makes sense for them to remain partners for a while—a few weeks or even a semester. In this way, you are able to have story partners form a bond with one another; this often adds to the depth of the discussion they can have.

Note-Taking—This is a very effective strategy for students who are at the end of second grade and older. Students can take notes at the very end of the mini-lesson, before independent reading time, or during the mini-lesson itself. Our students complete a short "Main Idea of the Mini-Lesson" page in their Companion Books right after dismissal from the meeting area. (See Jared's example of his week's worth of mini-lesson notes on page 46.) Keeping track of the mini-lesson is a great way for students to reflect on what they've been learning. It's an invaluable tool to use while communicating with parents. And it's immediately clear which students were successful and which students will need review.

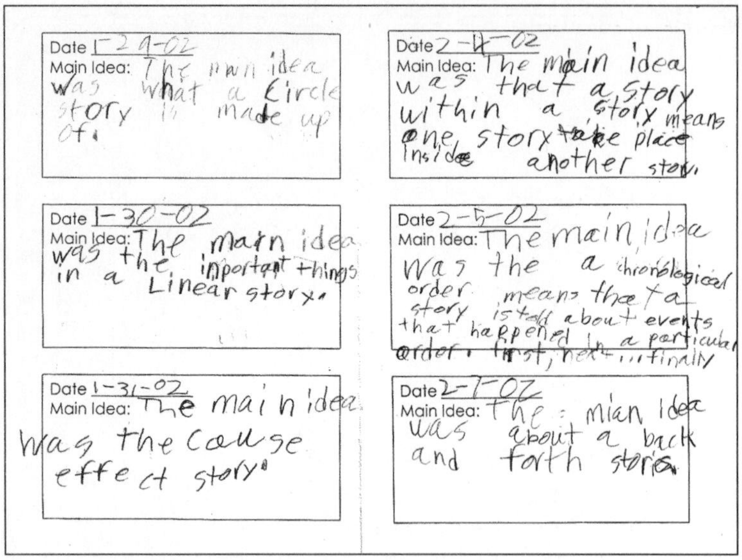

The handwritten journal entries at top:

Date 1-29-02
Main Idea: The own idea was what a circle story is made up of.

Date 2-4-02
Main Idea: The main idea was that a story within a story means one story take place inside another story.

Date 1-30-02
Main Idea: was the important things in a Linear story.

Date 2-5-02
Main Idea: was the a chronological order. means that a story is told about events that happened in a particular order. first, next...finally

Date 1-31-02
Main Idea: The main idea was the cause effect story.

Date 2-1-02
Main Idea: The mian idea was about a back and forth story.

Shared Reading—Here's a new twist on a familiar teaching concept. Shared reading is most beneficial during the mini-lesson/read aloud portion of the Workshop when you are working on oral reading skills and non-fiction strategies. During a shared reading lesson, you can use a big book or pass out copies of the book to each set of partners. You can use this read aloud time to practice reading fluently, reading to demonstrate punctuation use, and/or reading dialogue. For lessons with these kinds of purposes, it is a great help for the students to have a clear picture of the text.

In a non-fiction study, you might, for instance, have copies of a science article for each student. Ask students to gather with a clipboard and a highlighter. During the lesson, have the students watch as you glean important information from the text. Then, after discussion, let them try it on their own. Circulate among them much the same way you would if you were listening to "Story Partners" talk during the read aloud.

Although shared reading is not a technique to use very often, the mini-lesson/read aloud time is where it best fits into the Workshop format. In this case, the shared reading piece would become the read aloud for the day. You would not need to select an additional story to read to your students.

Ending the Mini-Lesson

Closure of a mini-lesson is of the utmost importance. Sending the kids off on the right foot helps to ensure their success during independent reading. We always like to end mini-lessons in the same way, with almost the same words each day. And we like to send them off with a mission, a task that will help them reflect on their own reading processes. For example, just before the lesson concludes, you might sum up for students how the new topic or concept will help them become better readers and then invite them to use (or find examples of) the day's topic in their own reading during the rest of the day.

Below we demonstrate successful endings for two different mini-lessons. In the first closing, the teacher urges students to apply a specific reading strategy; in the second example, students are asked to look for the elements of the story they are reading.

In the closing moments of a mini-lesson on the use of the "Questioning" strategy, you might hear a teacher saying something like,

Teacher: I'll bet that Eve Bunting would really want us to think about that question. By asking a question that compares our lives to the lives of the characters, we're able to get into the story a little bit more, which is exactly what good readers do, don't they? Today when you are reading, stop to ask yourself questions. Ask questions about what is happening, about why a character is doing something, about what something means. Really stop to notice when you have a question in your mind. When I meet with you in your book nook, there's a good chance that that will be the first thing I'll want to talk about: the questions in your mind. If you like, you may use your journal to write down some of your questions. When we meet at share time today, I'd like to talk about what's going on in your reading and what questions you asked while you were reading. All right readers, your book nooks are calling. Off you go!

In the closing moments of a mini-lesson on the story element of "change over time," you might hear a teacher say,

Teacher: From now on, when we talk about story elements, I'd like us to also talk about the changes that take place from beginning to end in our books. Let's add that right now to our story element chart. Let's add "changes over time" right underneath "solution." *(writes on chart)* Today in your book nook, if you are reading a fiction book, pay close attention to anything that might be changing during the story. Is a character changing his mind about something? Is a bad day changing into a good day? Be ready to share these changes with us at share time.

If you are working on something very concrete (like using strong words for "said" or using direct definition context clues), you may want to have students mark and write down where they found examples of the mini-lesson topic. For example, at the end of a mini-lesson on decoding words, we sometimes hand out two sticky notes to each student, instructing the students to write down any two words that they were able to figure out by finding the known chunks. At share time, we take the time to post each student's words on the board and talk about all the chunks we know that help us figure out bigger words. (Be sure to request that students hang on to their finds until share time. Otherwise, you may find that they all want to share with you right away what they found for themselves. One student's enthusiasm may detract from another's or from your own focus in group or conference.)

Ensuring a Smooth Transition to Independent Reading

Wasted minutes are a teacher's nightmare. We're always searching for ways to run the Reading Workshop more efficiently—especially the transition time from mini-lesson to book nooks. This is often the easiest time for kids to fall off track. You'll need to find a routine and stick with it. Think carefully about what will happen after the mini-lesson. Will you meet with a small group right away? Will it always be the same kids, or will it be a group that changes? Are you asking students to write about the mini-lesson before they go off to their book nooks? Depending on what will come next in your room, there are a few ways that dismissal from the meeting area can go quite smoothly.

Dismissing the whole class at once. This option works best if you are sending all students off right away to write about the mini-lesson in their journals. They'll finish their writing at different times, so there probably won't be a mass move to get a carpet square or to get their other book nook materials. It's helpful to use a particular phrase to focus students on the next task. We've had success with the phrase, "1, 2, 3, Read." We've taught the kids to know what each number means. When the teacher says "One," students are to zip their lips and look at the teacher. At "Two," students are to close their eyes and think about what they will write down about the mini-lesson. At "Three," they all stand quietly and face their desk. And at "Read," students move silently to their writing assignment. As they finish writing their thoughts, they get their own book nooks ready and begin their quiet reading. This whole process should take no more than five minutes. The predictability of the routine really helps students stay focused.

Dismissing small groups from the meeting area. This option works well only if you are sure you will be meeting with a certain group at the same time every day. If you plan to meet with your weaker readers for a guided reading lesson every day (and you certainly should!), you may want to meet with them right away. In that case, assign that group a name or a number and dismiss them with a task. For example, "Group one, please meet me at the reading table and begin your rereading of the book you took home last night." Once your group has begun, you can dismiss the other readers to their book nooks, reminding them to think about what they'll want to discuss when you meet with them for a reading conference.

Dismissing individuals to their reading or writing. We have used three different ways to dismiss students one at a time. Younger children, especially, enjoy the method of "secret code question." At the mini-lesson's end, you ask a question of all the students. Give them a moment to think about it and then call names one at a time. Students come up and whisper their answers in the teacher's ear. A correct answer, the "secret code," allows them to go off to their writing or to their book nook. An incorrect answer buys them another turn. The "secret code" dismissal becomes another opportunity for assessment in disguise!

Another simple dismissal technique is to distribute reading materials one at a time to students, allowing each student to leave when you hand out his or her journal or take-home reading book from the night before.

And finally, you may want to take advantage of the models in your room by signaling out those students who look ready to read. "Let me see. Jennifer can go off to her book nook. Who else is ready? Oh, John may leave…" Use whatever works!

Whichever routine you choose or work out for yourself, the key point to remember is what you don't want: everyone just getting up and going on to the next step without any clear directions. The calm, deliberate atmosphere that the mini-lesson helps to achieve would quickly disappear. It's important to ease into the next phase of the Workshop. The kids will pick up on your lead. They will see that it matters to you that everyone takes their time and that the room always feels like a working and thinking room.

In our Reading Workshops, the "icing on the mini-lesson cake" is the sign we hang outside as everyone makes their way to their book nooks. One special person each week hangs a sign that reads, "Quiet, please! We are reading!" on our door. It lets everyone know that we mean business, and we're ready to settle into another aspect of our reading lives, independent reading.

In Chapter Seven, we'll take an in-depth look at just what goes on during the independent reading phase. But first, let's continue with our discussion of successful mini-lessons. In the next three chapters we'll explore several kinds of Reading Workshop mini-lessons in greater detail.

CHAPTER 4

ESTABLISHING ROUTINES:
Mini-Lessons on Procedures

> "It's my job to put the 'Quiet' sign out when we start to read."
>
> —Madison, grade 3

W e've all experienced creating the exceptional lesson, well planned down to the ideal example and a sure-fire hands-on experiment. This is the lesson that could have been downright phenomenal—if only we hadn't forgotten to show students where to place finished papers or what to do if they finished early. Often it's these little behind-the-scenes procedures that can make or break any spectacular lesson.

The previous chapters began to examine some of the procedures that can help the Workshop run smoothly, every time, every day. However, these were teacher-initiated procedures. In this chapter, we'll look more closely at how to let the students in on the procedural secrets they need to know themselves. The emphasis here is on the direct teaching of those procedures students need to have in place before they can truly begin to grow as readers within the Reading Workshop.

The power of the Reading Workshop lies in the fact that it is so predictable. Students enter empowered, full of the feeling that they know what to expect. Sure, the story will change from day to day and, of course, there's always a new lesson. But students know that they will encounter a mini-lesson, book nooks, conference, writing, and sharing every day, in that order. Routine brings comfort. And comfort leads to learning.

September Is a Special Month in the Reading Workshop

We wholeheartedly recommend that teachers spend a great deal of time in September making sure Reading Workshop procedures are well ironed out. Our classes move slowly through the Workshop routines. In many Reading Workshop classrooms, students have been in school for almost a month before the entire Workshop is in place, working in real time.

While the first couple of days and weeks of the year hardly resemble a complete Reading Workshop, one component remains virtually unchanged from the first day of school to the last. That distinction belongs to the read aloud and mini-lesson. Mini-lessons act as the glue that holds the Reading Workshop together. Without them, the Workshop exists only as glorified quiet reading time. With them, students are guided daily through the reading process with the help of a competent reading teacher and coach. Mini-lessons should be taught every day, from the very first day of school to the very last. By selecting extremely entertaining read alouds right off the bat, you are able to set the tone of your Workshops for the entire year. For management purposes, you can phase in the other aspects of the Workshop slowly and carefully, but it's wise to make the power of the read aloud/mini-lesson work for you from day one.

> ### TEACHER to TEACHER
> In first grade, this first month of the Reading Workshop may occur in October or November. Younger students often need a little more time before they're ready for the independent reading that is so necessary to Reading Workshop success.

Four Weeks of Lessons to Phase In the Reading Workshop

Each year we move our classes through the procedural steps at different rates. When thinking about how to effectively begin your Workshop, you'll need to consider the maturity, grade level, and previous experiences of your students. Younger students need lots of modeling and practice of appropriate book nook behaviors. Older students require as much modeling and practice with journal response. Take a look at how a second-grade teacher and a fourth-grade teacher view their Reading Workshop goals in the beginning of the year.

EXAMPLES OF READING WORKSHOP PROCEDURAL MINI-LESSONS

- Workshop introduction
- Workshop rules and expectations
- Appropriate Workshop/book nook voices
- Listening skills
- Choosing book nooks and book nook behavior
- Seeking help during book nook time
- Book choice—choosing a just right book
- Reading conferences—the role of the teacher and the role of the student
- Keeping and storing records
- Giving book talks
- Taking care of books and the classroom library
- Reading with a partner or small group
- Discussion with a partner or small group
- Responding to the text—journal entries
- Abandoning a book
- Take-home books, homework journals, and homework assignments
- Respecting the Reading Workshop and other readers

WEEKLY GOALS FOR THE SECOND-GRADE WORKSHOP

Week One:

Reading Workshop Total Time: *30 minutes*

- Teach mini-lessons that introduce students to the Workshop model, appropriate behaviors, book nook selection.

- Have students move from the mini-lesson to places around the room. Practice movement and transitions.

- Practice being in the book nook for a short period of time. Monitor behavior and reward as necessary.

Week Two:

Reading Workshop Total Time: *45 minutes*

- Choose mini-lessons that transition to short (10–15 minute) book nook time.

- Focus on making sure students are quiet and aware of what to do should they need something.

- Have students return to the meeting area. Model journal writing response to the story read at mini-lesson time. Students should know that in a few days, they will be responding in a similar way to the book they were reading in book nooks.

Week Three:

Reading Workshop Total Time: *55 minutes*

- Use mini-lessons that transition to longer quiet reading time (15–20 minutes).

- Hold conferences focusing mostly on choosing just right books and appropriate behaviors.

- After reading time, have students return to their desks for modeling and guided practice of any record keeping.

- Ask students to move back to meeting area so that you can continue to model journal writing responses.

RECOMMENDED BOOKS FOR MINI-LESSONS ON PROCEDURES AND ROUTINES

Workshop Introduction and Routine

The Bee Tree by Patricia Polacco

Edward and the Pirates by David McPhail

I Hate to Read by Rita Marshall

Running the Road to ABC by Denize Lauture

A Story for Bear by Dennis Haseley

The Way to Start a Day by Byrd Baylor

Wolf! by Becky Bloom

Workshop Rules

David Goes to School by David Shannon

Lily's Purple Plastic Purse by Kevin Henkes

Appropriate Workshop Voices

Mortimer by Robert Munsch

Listening Skills

Listen Buddy by Helen Lester

Peter Rabbit by Beatrix Potter

Book Choice

Goldilocks and the Three Bears by James Marshall

Goldilocks and the Three Hares by Heidi Petach

Choosing a Place to Read

The Best Place to Read by Debbie Bertram and Susan Bloom

Humphrey's Corner by Sally Hunter

Me on the Map by Joan Sweeny

My Map Book by Sara Fanelli

A Quiet Place by Douglas Wood

Taking Care of a Book

Library Dragon by Carmen Agra Deedy

Library Lil by Suzanne Williams

More Than Anything Else by Marie Bradby

Richard Wright and the Library Card by William Miller

📖 Lay the foundation for share time and encourage students to bring something from quiet reading time to meeting area to share.

Week Four:

Reading Workshop Total Time: *All allotted time*

📖 Teach mini-lessons that transition to quiet reading time for the full time allowed.

📖 Hold small groups and continue with individual reading conferences.

📖 Have students return to seats for record keeping. Assist as necessary.

📖 Ask students to create written responses of what they read independently. Carefully monitor and intervene where necessary.

📖 Have students meet for share time.

In the primary grades, it's important to focus on helping students make smooth transitions because frequent movement is a part of the Reading Workshop at this stage. Moving fluidly and without disruption helps younger students stay focused and on task. In the upper grades, the Reading Workshop requires less movement and less frequent use of book nooks. Most students write while they read. Transitioning, then, is less of an issue. As you'll see in the following example, you can spend time with upper elementary students best by modeling written responses and making all Workshop expectations clear.

WEEKLY GOALS FOR THE FOURTH-GRADE WORKSHOP

Week One:

Reading Workshop Total Time: *30 minutes*

📖 Teach procedural mini-lessons that transition to shortened quiet reading time.

📖 Use a checklist of appropriate reading behaviors.

📖 Allow students time to browse in the library and complete reading surveys.

📖 Monitor and reward for acceptable behaviors.

📖 Have students meet back in mini-lesson area. Model possible journal response using the read aloud from the mini-lesson.

Week Two:

Reading Workshop Total Time: *45 minutes*

📖 Teach mini-lessons that transition to longer book nook time.

📖 Hold short conferences that focus on book choice.

📖 Have students begin to respond in journals as they read.

📖 Continue to model for students what appropriate journals look like.

Week Three:

Reading Workshop Total Time: *50 minutes*

📖 Teach mini-lessons that address grading expectations. Share Reading Workshop rubric and journal rubrics.

📖 Teach mini-lessons that transition to full time quiet reading.

📖 Hold conferences that focus on appropriate book choice and written responses.

📖 Have students meet for share time.

Week Four:

Reading Workshop Total Time: *60 minutes (or all allotted time)*

📖 Teach mini-lessons that transition to book nooks for the full time allotted.

📖 Hold small skill groups as needed.

📖 Hold conferences that focus on book choice, written responses, and reading strategies.

📖 Make sure share time is polished. Allow ample time to discuss expectations of speakers and listeners. Use of a share time checklist is helpful.

SAMPLE PROCEDURAL MINI-LESSON ON SELECTING A BOOK NOOK

Very early in the year, our students know the importance of book nooks. This mini-lesson took place in the second week of school in a third-grade classroom. For the lesson, we selected the book *Humphrey's Corner* by Sally Hunter. The book follows a young character, Humphrey, who searches for a "just right" place to play. We like the simple connection between a place to play and a place to read.

Teacher: Boys and Girls, it's so exciting to be getting our Reading Workshop off the ground. I can tell that you are ready to become spectacular readers. As you know, after we do the mini-lesson and read aloud, all of you will go off to special places in the room we call our book nooks. It's really important that we select a place in the room that helps us concentrate on our reading. I've found a book to share with you about a little elephant who is searching for a just right place to play. Not every place in his house is a good place to play. And that reminds me of our book nooks. Not every place in the classroom is a good place to read. Let's read and find out what happens.

(Teacher begins to read the story)

Teacher: What does it seem Humphrey is searching for?

Student: He wants an interesting place to play with his toys.

T: Yes, he does. Has that ever happened to you? Have you ever had to search out a good place to play?

(Various responses from the class)

T: *(Continues to read story)* Humphrey is trying all sorts of different places. Why isn't he staying put in one place?

S: It seems there's one or two things about each place that he doesn't like.

S: Yeah, like the bathroom floor was too hard and his mom's bedroom was too dark.

S: He's looking for a perfect place!

S: This is reminding me of *Goldilocks and the Three Bears*.

T: I can see how you would make that connection. Yes, Humphrey doesn't want to play just anywhere. He's really searching for a place that will make him comfortable and safe—a good place for playing with his toys. Let's keep reading to see how it ends. *(Continues to read.)*

T: Now, boys and girls, we are not just like Humphrey. We are not going to find a spot in the room that would make a good place to play. But we are like Humphrey because we need to find a spot in the room that is just right...for reading! What do you think would make a spot a good place for your book nook?

S: Over by the window?

T: Yes, I agree. Why do you think that spot would make a good book nook?

S: Because it's got a pillow.

S: Because it's got lots of light.

S: Because there's only room for one person, so you won't stop to talk to a friend.

T: Those are all great characteristics of a good book nook. I'm going to list those on our chart right here—"Good Book Nooks...are comfortable, are well lighted, are private." Can anyone else give another example of a good book nook around the room?

S: How about underneath the computer desk?

T: Well, no. That is not a book nook because of all the wires there. It's unsafe to be under that table. I'm going to add that to the chart, "Good Book Nooks are...safe." But you may wish to read under a different table that does not have any wires. Any other possible book nook ideas?

S: How about using the carpet squares from the library?

T: Yes, that's an excellent idea. You can put a carpet square in lots of different places in the room. Watch me for a moment as I walk around the room and show you exactly where you can and cannot choose. Be thinking about where you'd like to have your own book nook. *(Teacher moves around the room and shows students areas that are off limits and areas that are good choices).* Now boys and girls, let's take a few minutes and act like Humphrey. Let's all walk around and try out a few places. Remember, you're looking for places that are comfortable, well lighted, private, and safe. You're looking for places that will help you concentrate on your book.

(Students try out various book nooks, while the teacher approves or redirects. Depending on the time, students may bring a book for a few minutes of quiet reading.)

Twenty Days of Mini-Lessons

In the remainder of this chapter, we present a plan for mini-lessons that encompasses the first month of the Reading Workshop. Only minor modifications are needed for each grade level. For each day, we provide a possible lesson topic and rationale for presenting the lesson, as well as supportive teacher talk and other notes that are helpful in elaborating the message of each procedural mini-lesson.

Day 1

FAVORITE BOOK SHARING: *This beginning lesson sets the tone that reading is and will continue to be very important to the class.*

"We are going to learn a lot about ourselves as readers. By sharing the books we already love, we'll get to know each other a little bit better."

This is a great way to start off the year. See the sample "back-to-school" letter encouraging students to bring their favorite book on the very first day of school.

Dear _____,

Hello, hello, hello! I'm very excited to be your third-grade teacher this year. I know that we will have exciting adventures together.

I hope that you have had a great summer. But now it's time for me (and you) to start thinking about school again. I hope that you can come to visit me in your new classroom during James River's Open House on Friday, August 31st from 1:00 – 3:00. You'll get to write me a letter and tell me what you've been up to, pick out your cubby, and maybe even meet some new classmates!

But here's the most important reason for this letter…your homework. Yup! It's that time again. I am so looking forward to starting our reading journey together that I want us to start that very first day of school by sharing a favorite book. So, when you get your bookbag ready with all of your new supplies for the first day of school, be sure to include your favorite book. It could be a book you have read or a book someone has read to you. I can't wait to see what kinds of books you bring to share. Can you guess what mine will be? Here's a hint…it's about a little boy at the bottom of a well.

Enjoy the rest of the summer! I'll see you soon.

Love,

Day 2

WHAT GOOD LISTENERS DO: *All students must be able to listen thoughtfully to conversations about literature.*

"Every day before I begin the mini-lesson, I will need to see your body language telling me, 'I am ready!' We won't get started until everyone looks and acts ready."

The use of classroom charts with rules for listening is very appropriate here. It's also helpful to create a chart entitled, "What a good listener looks like and sounds like."

Good literature makes it even easier for students to practice good listening skills.

Day 3

OUR READING WORKSHOP: AN INTRODUCTION: *Give students a "big picture" of what their Workshop will be like. Explain how it might be different from what they are used to. Build excitement!*

"We will be working together this year to become excellent readers and thinkers. We'll do this in our Reading Workshop. Let's look at what our schedule will look like once we've got all the pieces together. Remember though, it will take some time to get the Workshop working the way we want it."

Refer to a copy (or poster) of your Reading Workshop schedule.

Day 4

INTRODUCTION TO QUIET READING AND BOOK NOOKS: *Most students have had some experience with silent reading time. However, you need to make clear that the Reading Workshop's quiet reading time is a bit different. For instance, you'll be around to conference with students about their individual reading.*

"One of the best things you'll get to do in our Reading Workshop is pick out your own books for reading time. You may read by yourself or maybe with a partner. And, you may find a place other than your desk to do your reading. When I read, I sure do get pretty comfortable! While you're reading I might be around to conference with you about the reading work that you are doing. That's how we'll work together to help you become a strong, thinking reader."

Define and discuss book nooks at this point. Give the students time to "mosey" around the room and select a possible place for their book nook. Have students "practice" reading in their book nooks. Point out the acceptable behaviors: "I love the way Sarah's eyes are in her book…I can tell she's being a reader." Reconvene as a class to create another reference chart entitled, "Book Nook Dos and Don'ts."

Day 5

READING WORKSHOP RULES: *Oh, what a perfect world it would be if everyone did what they were supposed to do! Here's your chance to be totally explicit about your expectations. Students need to know that precious reading minutes are at stake.*

"We have rules in our classroom in order to keep everyone safe and to make our classroom a friendly place to learn. Rules at reading time will be no different. It is absolutely necessary that you do not waste any of your reading time. Why would you want to?"

If you are using a behavior component in your Workshop, this is a good time to discuss it. It's also a good idea to have copies of the rules for students to keep with their reading materials.

Day 6

CARING FOR BOOKS AND THE CLASSROOM LIBRARY: *While it is true that books do fall apart after a while, every person in the Workshop needs to make sure this doesn't happen often. This lesson often takes more than one day; you'll probably refer to its main points all year long.*

"We are so lucky to have so many wonderful books to read and share with one another. However, having these books comes with a responsibility. We must take good care of each book. We want our library to grow with new titles, not with replacements of titles we've already had but ruined."

Depending on the grade level, you may need to go in depth, perhaps do some role-playing if necessary. With older students, this would be the appropriate time to discuss how they will check out and return books from the library. Also, if possible, meet near your classroom library. Discuss how it's organized and what each class member can do to be sure it stays that way.

Day 7

APPROPRIATE WORKSHOP VOICES: *A Reading Workshop room feels different. All students are not engaged in the same activity, yet they are all engaged. Some students will need to concentrate on their own independent reading; some students will need to work with a partner; and some will be in a small group, with or without the teacher. While the room is not absolutely silent, the noise level should be conducive to all of these activities.*

"I love to hear you guys outside on the playground. Your excited voices tell me you're having a blast. But how do you think I might feel if I heard those same loud voices in our Reading Workshop? It's very important for us to remember that there are twenty other readers in the room. Even if you are in a group, or with a partner, there is still someone else who needs quiet to concentrate. We need to work hard to make sure everyone has the quiet they deserve in order to help us all grow as readers. Let's practice using those quiet, reading voices now…"

An excellent way to introduce this concept is to take a "field trip" to your school's cafeteria and library. Ask students to notice what they observed about the sounds in those places. Lead them to see the rationale behind a quiet work environment.

Day 8

CHOOSING A JUST RIGHT BOOK: *Independent reading is only effective to the extent that students are actively engaged in reading a book at their independent level. When the book is too hard, the student is probably doing too much "reading work" to make sense of the whole. When the book is too easy, not enough reading work is being done to stretch the reader's abilities.*

"One of the things we will talk a lot about this year is 'just right' books. We are all at different places in our reading. And that's just fine, because we are all very different people. What works for Jonathan may not work for Terry. That's just the way it is. Your job in Reading Workshop is to choose a book that is not too hard and not too easy. You need to pick a book that is just right! That's what will help you to be a better reader, reading just right books."

A weight-lifting analogy works great here. Tell students that you are trying to build up your muscles. Will you go into a gym and pick up the teeniest, tiniest weight there is? Will you just try and lift the heaviest weight there? No, in order to build your muscles, you'll pick a weight that's not too light and not too heavy. It's exactly the same with reading muscles. It's important to share your own reading with students. Show them what is just right for you and what is too difficult for you to read all the time...a physics book from the library perhaps!

Day 9

MAPPING OUT BOOK NOOKS: *Book nooks work best if everyone has a set spot in the room that he or she goes to every day. It adds to the predictability of the Workshop. A map of the classroom helps students remember their place and see the importance of the routine.*

"We've talked together about what book nooks are, and you've even tried out a few of them for yourself. Today we're going to find one special place that you can call your very own book nook for some time. Let's all go now and find a place that feels right. I have a map here of our classroom. If I agree that you have selected a good book nook, I'll chart it on our map so that we'll be able to refer to it later."

Be sure to emphasize that the map can, and will, be changed if needed—and that being in a book nook is a privilege, not a right.

> **TEACHER to TEACHER**
> This is a wonderful lesson to tie in to a social studies and geography lesson about maps. For this lesson, we love the book Me on the Map by Joan Sweeney. We make lots of connections between the maps in the books and a map that we create of our own classroom. Students then write their names on small sticky notes, find book nooks in the room, and return to the classroom map to put their names in the appropriate spots to "claim their book nooks."

Day 10

STRATEGIES FOR CHOOSING BOOKS:
Students will need a bag of tricks to rely on when faced with the shelves of the library. At this point, they already know that they need to be reading just right books. Now they can learn how to choose one!

"Let's talk about specific ways you can tell if a book is just right for you or not. Have you ever heard of the five-finger test? Let me describe it to you. (See Teacher to Teacher tip box at right.) So, when you are searching for a just right book, be sure to refer to the chart hanging in the library. Remember, it's the just right books that will exercise your reading muscles and make them grow!"

Create—and/or share—a chart of Book Choosing Strategies. (See the example on page 61 for strategies on how to choose a just right book.)

> **TEACHER to TEACHER**
> To conduct the five-finger test, a student randomly chooses one page in the text. For every unknown word, she puts up one finger. If she has 5 fingers up before the end of the page, the book is too hard. We also like to include a comprehension check. After the student reads the one page, she retells it in her own words. If she can retell it, she gives a thumbs up—it's a just right book. This variation is the "five finger and a thumb test." In first grade, you may want to modify this to the two- or three-finger test to accommodate the very few words on each page of beginning texts.

- Think about your purpose for reading today. Are you reading to find out something or reading for enjoyment?

- Think about what types of books you enjoy reading. Or think about finding a genre you haven't read lately.

- Read the back cover.

- Read the inside flaps.

- Read any reviews on the first couple of pages.

- Talk to a friend who has read it before.

- Read the first page. Does it hook you?

- See if it reminds you of another book you have read and enjoyed.

- Choose a page from the middle and do a five-finger test.

- Now do a five-finger and a thumb test to see if you can retell a part of the page you read in your own words.

- Take a picture walk through the book.

- Read the Table of Contents.

- Have you read another book in the same series?

- Did you hear the book read out loud?

Day 11

READING CONFERENCES: *For conferences to be most effective, students need to know why you hold conferences and what happens during a conference. Again, this adds to the predictability of the Workshop.*

"I would like you to get a sneak peak into what will happen when I come to sit and read with you. This is called a reading conference. Both of us have important jobs that we need to do in the reading conference. Let's take a look at what happens in a reading conference together. (Refer to the conferencing chart on page 62.) Remember, my job at this time is to help you grow as a reader. I'll expect you to listen to the advice I give you in the reading conference."

If possible, teach this mini-lesson with another adult role-playing the part of a student in the conference. Let the class see what you will be doing and what they are expected to do. (See the sample lesson on page 41.)

Day 12

HELP ME: *Students should not be bothering you during a reading group or conference. This is sacred time. They need to know what they should do if they need assistance.*

"Readers, I want you to understand that when I am in a reading conference or group with other readers, I do not want to be interrupted. You all deserve that time with me, and I don't want anything to bother us while we are working together. Let's work together now to make a plan so we all know what to do if you need something."

Brainstorm together all the things that might happen during independent reading time (bathroom breaks, inability to find a book, stuck on a word, etc.) and the possible ways a student might solve the problem without interrupting you.

Day 13

READING WORKSHOP OFFICE WORK: *Depending on the grade level, students should be responsible for varying degrees of maintaining reading records—main idea sheets, reading logs, journal entries, etc. Students need to learn what to maintain and how best to maintain it.*

"One of my jobs as teacher is to keep good records. I need to write down my plans, notes about what I do, and fill out lots of paper work for the office. I am responsible for all of these things. You have a similar job as a reader in our Reading Workshop. You have some paperwork—office work—to do as well. Let's take a look at what you're responsible for."

Have available overheads or sample pages of any forms you will require students to maintain. Model and post the correct way this is to be done. Then, take some time and have students practice recording and filing the forms appropriately and accurately.

Days 14 and 15

POSSIBLE BOOK RESPONSES AND JOURNAL WRITING: *Over the year, students will develop a keen sense of literature response. As the Workshop gets off the ground, they need to internalize the concept that books make us think and that we should stop to reflect on those thoughts, sometimes on our own and sometimes with a friend.*

"When I finish reading a book I never just slam the book shut and move on to another. I sit for minute and think about the book. I may even call up a friend and recommend the book to him or her. One of the things you'll be doing with the books that you are reading is responding to them. What do you remember about your reading? What did it make you think of? I want to know the thoughts that are in your head as you read. Our reading journals will become a map of our thoughts, the place where we can record all the adventures on which books have taken us."

During the read aloud, stop often to emphasize the thinking you are doing. Plant the seeds for response. After (or during, depending on the level), model the response journal you are expecting. Then, take a few minutes to create a list of possible things to say after a day's reading. Push students to see that you would like to see some details of the book but also evidence of their own thinking. Plan on modeling appropriate journal responses often during the next few weeks.

Day 16

SHARE TIME: *Share time is an invaluable way for students to get to know each other as readers. Books, strategies, and enthusiasm spread from child to child at this time.*

"Do you recall that I told you yesterday what I do when I finish a book? I call a friend. I love to share what I've just read. You will have an opportunity to do the same each day. You'll have a chance to show classmates what you learned, what you thought was funny, what you think others should read...anything you want to tell us about your reading today. Share time is when we'll get to find out what everyone's been doing with their time in book nooks."

Think about how you would like your students to share. Will they sign up to do so? Will there be a consistent, rotating schedule? Share the procedure with students during this mini-lesson. Recall the mini-lesson on listening and again emphasize its importance.

> ### TEACHER to TEACHER
> Due to time constraints, it's not possible for everyone to share each day. However, in order to give everyone an opportunity to share occasionally, have students pair up and share with a buddy. Pairs of students sit quietly together and talk about their reading work. After a few minutes of sharing with each other, some of the pairs can share what they learned from each other.

Day 17

GIVING A BOOK TALK: *Good books are often contagious. Students enjoy helping others find a new book. A strong book talk by a student helps to keep books off the shelves and in students' hands—right where they belong!*

"When I finish a great book, I often find someone else who would like to read it. I love the feeling I get when someone comes back to me and says, 'You were right, that was a wonderful book!' I'd like to show you today what to do if you finish a super book that you think other students in our class might enjoy."

It's helpful to have a pre-determined outline of what you want your students to include in their book talk. Book talks are more like commercials than book reports. They're short, to the point, and often end with a cliffhanger to "hook" the audience. Give a few example book talks and show students how and when they'll be able to share their own book talks. Allow students to practice giving book talks with books the class has read together.

Day 18

BRINGING ALL THE PIECES TOGETHER/TROUBLE SHOOTING: *It's hard work getting all of the components of the Reading Workshop together. Students may need a reminder of what the big picture really is. And they may also need time just to ask questions about what their jobs are.*

"I am so proud of the work we have done together getting our Workshop all set up. Let's take a few minutes to talk about what you expect to happen every day. Does anyone have any questions about the Reading Workshop? Let's take some time to look at the schedule again... Now, let's see if we can run through the whole Workshop together."

Have a "pretend mini-lesson" and dismiss students afterward. Let them go through the motions, praising and coaching them as needed. Let students practice being in the book nooks long enough to make sure there are no more kinks to work out and continue with the run-through. At "pretend share time" you may want to have some sort of mini-celebration. "Yeah! We have a working Workshop." Perhaps give out new bookmarks or pencils for reading journals. Then, by all means, go back to book nooks for reading time!

Day 19

READING WITH A PARTNER: *Students often love to share their reading with a partner. When it's done correctly, it can be a great learning opportunity for both partners. It is essential to take the time up front to show students how (and where and how often) they will be permitted to read with a partner.*

"A few days ago, we talked about how wonderful it is to share what we are reading with other students. Sometimes, it's even fun to read the same book together with another student. Just as with everything else in Reading Workshop, there's a right way to do this. Let's talk about the dos and don'ts of reading with a partner."

See Chapter 7 for more detailed information about reading with partners.

Day 20

THE (RIGHT) WAY TO HAVE A READING WORKSHOP: *This lesson is inspired by Byrd Baylor's book,* The Way To Start a Day. *We like to ceremonially end the first month by saying, "We are ready for our Reading Workshop in its entirety."*

"Readers, we have come so far with our Workshop. I am so excited about using all of our Workshop time as readers and thinkers. Let's take one last look at what our jobs are, what you expect and what I expect of our Reading Workshop time."

Younger students especially enjoy partner reading. It quickly becomes a favorite part of the Workshop.

THE WAY TO HAVE A READING WORKSHOP

- Gather together for a good story and to learn some tips on being a good reader.
- Listen carefully and thoughtfully.
- Stay in your own book nook or at your desk.
- Read quietly in book nooks. Be careful not to disturb other readers.
- Think about what you would like to talk about in your next reading conference.
- Think about what you would like to share with other readers.
- Keep track of all reading materials.
- Keep the library and materials areas neat for other readers to use.
- Read, read, read!

After reading the book, we create one final procedural chart entitled, "The Way to Have a Reading Workshop." Many charts come and go throughout the year, but this one stays, all year long.

CHAPTER 5

PURSUING MEANING:

Mini-Lessons on Reading Strategies and Skills

> "I need to practice my reading so I can get better."
> —Joel, grade 1

As adults, we read for many different reasons and purposes. For pleasure and relaxation, we settle in front of a fire with a novel. To assist us in our own personal and career growth, we delve into professional books and journals. Or we target a specific expository piece as we prepare new content to teach. We choose books according to these different purposes and read in a way that suits our needs, engaging in certain reading behaviors and utilizing helpful strategies as we read.

We need to think of ourselves as readers as we consider our students. If the goal of reading is to be an independent reader and thinker, then the mini-lessons that focus on reading strategies and skills are probably the most important lessons you can teach. We all want our students to derive the same satisfaction from reading as we ourselves do: to be strategic and skillful readers, to be able to understand what they are reading, and to know what to do when they have difficulty. In order to use appropriate reading strategies and skills effectively, students need to personally observe their teacher demonstrating these reading behaviors. Thus, modeling and direct teaching are critical.

This chapter provides background information on what we feel are the most important strategies and skills to teach. We take you into our classrooms to "see" these lessons in action by offering examples of mini-lessons on strategies and skills and sharing with you a wealth of children's literature to accompany these lessons.

Reading Strategies and Skills Instruction

Reading strategies are the "in-the-head processes" that readers use to make sense out of print (Pearson, et. al., 1992). When we read, so much is going on in our heads. We make connections between the book and our own life; we get pictures in our minds of events in the story; we ask ourselves questions when we're confused; and we infer meaning from the text when we feel the author hasn't told us everything.

Students need to know what expert readers do before, during, and after reading. By demonstrating reading strategies, you can show them what needs to occur throughout their own reading process. It is essential that they see you questioning, rereading, and adjusting your rate of speed so that they can develop a consciousness—called metacognition—of what they are doing. This is true even of capable readers, who are often not consciously aware of the strategies that they are using. For instance, typically these readers don't realize that they automatically re-read when something doesn't make sense.

But it is the reluctant readers who especially benefit from a teacher's modeling. These readers often simply give up when they encounter difficulty, such as an unknown word or a confusing paragraph. They don't use the strategies that more able readers use because they don't know what to do. You need to let these less able readers in on the secrets. These readers need to know what good readers do when they encounter difficulty or confusion. And less able readers must see that good readers, too, have reading problems and need to employ fix-up strategies.

By demonstrating reading behaviors and then monitoring those of your students, you can observe whether they apply these strategies in their independent reading. At the same time, let the students know that they will be held accountable for these strategies.

Because they help readers to construct meaning, reading strategies are essential. However, reading skills are also needed to understand the text. Skills are usually viewed as the more specific and mechanical aspects of reading—such as sequencing, cause and effect, skimming a passage for specific information, comparing and contrasting, and adjusting reading rate. (Fountas and Pinnell, 2001). Reading skills also encompass a myriad of study tools, such as the ability to use text features to understand expository text, the ability to locate information from sources, or the correct use of a book's index. A note of caution here: In the past, reading and study skills have too often been assigned as solitary worksheets. Students need to learn both skills and strategies with real books and materials, not with workbooks and worksheets.

The Importance of Mini-Lessons on Reading Strategies and Skills

The best time to offer direct instruction on strategies and skills, and to model their use for your students, is during the mini-lesson.

For example, through a mini-lesson's read aloud or the lesson portion itself, you can:

- 📖 use books like *Tar Beach* by Faith Ringgold, *Dear Willie Rudd* by Libba Moore Gray, or *When Jessie Came Across the Sea* by Amy Hest to model for your students how to make effective inferences.

- 📖 decide that a lesson on "re-reading to clarify" is necessary for students who are reading nonfiction material and who need to be shown how to re-read new information or confusing parts for clarification. This may also be an appropriate lesson for a small group of students having difficulty understanding what they've read.

- have mini-lessons on skills like identifying the main idea of a story. Books such as *The Great Kapok Tree* by Lynne Cherry or *Stellaluna* by Jannell Cannon are particularly suited for this topic.

- teach sequencing by demonstrating the order of the ingredients in *Stone Soup* by Marcia Brown.

Careful and regular observations of your students will allow you to make these and other instructional decisions.

The skills and strategy mini-lessons presented in this chapter are not intended to be lessons that are only taught once. These lessons are most effective when they are returned to over and over again during the course of the year.

Mini-Lesson Lesson Plan for Strategy and Skill Instruction

Good instruction is a result of good planning. Teachers need to provide lessons that will make a genuine difference in students' reading. That requires taking the time to think through and plan your lesson. The following four steps will help you plan your strategy and skill instruction.

1. DETERMINE WHAT STRATEGY OR SKILL NEEDS TO BE TAUGHT

Assess your students:

- Are they making predictions?

- Can they infer meaning from passages?

- Do they reread confusing material?

- Are they able to recall the main ideas as well as the details?

2. PLAN A LESSON TO TEACH A STRATEGY OR SKILL

Develop a plan for your mini-lesson:

- Determine your purpose for the lesson.

- Choose a read aloud that you can use for this purpose.

- Consider the reading process. What do you want to cover before (some hook), during (a think aloud) and after reading (restate/discuss).

- Determine what materials you might want to use to support your lesson.

- Provide questions for discussion.

3. FOLLOW-UP THE LESSON

Encourage your students to apply the strategy or skill:

- Consider how to assist students in applying this strategy or skill to their personal reading (through conferences and partner reading).

- Have students write in their journal about their application of the lesson to their independent reading.

📖 Decide how much more time should be spent on this particular strategy or skill.

📖 Allow for follow-up lessons for smaller groups of students.

📖 Consider how you can continue to remind students to use this strategy or skill even after you finish "teaching" it.

4. EVALUATE

When conferring with students, determine:

📖 The successful application of the strategy or skill.

📖 How the students are applying the strategy or skill as determined by the journal or when viewed in conference.

📖 Which students still need support.

First-grade boys apply strategies and skills they have learned in recent mini-lessons.

Developing Mini-Lessons on Reading Comprehension Strategies

Proficient readers make appropriate book choices and actively engage in their reading. They derive meaning from the text because they bring their own personal experiences and background knowledge to their reading. These readers are using key strategies as they interact with text; as a teacher, you want all of your students to have these rewarding reading experiences (Harvey and Goudvis, 2000; Keene and Zimmerman, 1997; Pearson, et.al., 1992).

To help you provide strong strategy learning experiences, we offer here extensive lists of topics and books for teaching strategies. In addition, at the end of this section, we share a sample mini-lesson on making connections.

Topics for Mini-Lessons on Reading Strategies

A detailed list of possible topics for mini-lessons on strategies follows on page 69. The first eight strategies are marked with an asterisk (*); these are key strategies that have sample lesson plans included later in this chapter. These are the strategies that you want to be sure your students are using regularly and automatically as they read.

Recommended Books for Mini-Lessons on Reading Strategies

The list on page 70 includes books that we use regularly for teaching reading strategies. Although it is an extensive list, it is not exhaustive. We have tried to include those books that are favorites for us, most of which are picture storybooks. Picture books are effective for teaching strategies, for intermediate as well as primary grades, because they offer a complete story in one reading. We also have included a number of chapter books that are appropriate for some of the strategies. The more challenging stories or chapter books are boldfaced in the list.

Extended Sample Reading Strategy Mini-Lesson

While working with a group of second and third graders, we decided to focus on the strategy of getting the students to make connections from the text to their own lives. We knew they would understand the story better if they could identify with the character's problems.

Making Connections from Text to Self

DAY 1: READ ALOUD AND STRATEGY INTRODUCTION

We chose several books to read aloud to show students how we make connections as we read. The first book we read was *Wemberley Worried* by Kevin Henkes. In this story, Wemberley worries about everything. She becomes especially anxious when school begins. We chose this book because we thought most students might have some experience with being nervous or worried. We started out by talking about things we worry about, things that make us nervous. We talked about getting nervous when school begins in the fall, not only when we were little but even now as teachers.

As Marybeth read the book, she stopped and pointed out connections she made. Wemberley carries a stuffed rabbit and rubs the ears as she gets worried, and Marybeth talked about stuffed animals she had that helped her. By the end of the book Wemberley meets a friend who is very similar in behavior to her. Marybeth talked about how she felt meeting new friends at school and asked our students how they felt when they made friends. Throughout the book, she showed the students how you can make connections to your life and how that can help you better understand what you read.

STRATEGIC READING MINI-LESSON TOPICS

◆ "Looking Ahead" strategies:* previewing a book, setting a purpose for reading, using background knowledge and personal experiences

◆ "Fix-Up" Strategies:* rereading to clarify, skipping ahead, using context and syntax, identifying confusing parts, identifying confusing vocabulary

◆ Making Connections:* text to self, text to text, text to world

◆ Questioning*

◆ Visualizing*

◆ Making Inferences*

◆ "Making It Your Own" strategies:* summarizing and synthesizing

◆ "Looking Back" strategies:* reflecting

◆ Determining important ideas and details

◆ Self-monitoring comprehension

◆ Making, evaluating, and adjusting predictions

◆ Pausing to recall details

◆ Drawing conclusions

◆ Summarizing and paraphrasing

◆ Finding evidence to support thinking

◆ Thinking aloud

RECOMMENDED BOOKS FOR TEACHING STRATEGY MINI-LESSONS

Looking Ahead

Previewing a book and making predictions

Dr. White by Jane Goodall

If You Give a Mouse a Cookie by Laura Numeroff

Ira Sleeps Over by Bernard Waber

Just Plain Fancy by Patricia Polacco

Pink and Say by Patricia Polacco

Sarah Plain and Tall by Patricia MacLachlan

Background knowledge or personal experience

Finding the Titanic by Robert D. Ballard

Fireflies by Julie Brinckloe

The Raft by Jim LeMarche

Stellaluna by Janell Cannon

Verdi by Janell Cannon

When I Was Young in the Mountains by Cynthia Rylant

Fix-Up Strategies

Bridge to Terabithia by Katherine Paterson

Dory Story by Jerry Pallotta

Pets in Trumpets by Bernard Most

Shiloh by Phyllis Reynolds Naylor

There's an Ant in Anthony by Bernard Most

Top of the World: Climbing Mt. Everest by Steve Jenkins

Tuck Everlasting by Natalie Babbitt

When Jessie Came Across the Sea by Amy Hest

Making Connections

Text to self

Alexander and the Terrible, Horrible, No Good, Very Bad Day by Judith Viorst

Andrew's Loose Tooth by Robert Munsch

Ballerinas Don't Wear Glasses by Ainslie Manson and Dean Griffiths

Canoe Days by Gary Paulsen

Fireflies by Julie Brinckloe

Gettin' Through Thursday by Melrose Cooper

Ira Sleeps Over by Bernard Waber

Koala Lou by Mem Fox

Lily's Purple Plastic Purse by Kevin Henkes

Lizzy and Skunk by Marie-Louise Fitzpatrick

Max's Dragon Shirt by Rosemary Wells

Memory Box by Mary Bahr

Memory String by Eve Bunting

Miss Malarkey Doesn't Live in Room 10 by Judy Finchler

My Rotten Red-Headed Older Brother by Patricia Polacco

The Pain and the Great One by Judy Blume

Sick Day by Patricia MacLachlan

Sidewalk Story by Sharon Bell Mathis

Thunder Cake by Patricia Polacco

Up North at the Cabin by Marsha Wilson Chall

War with Grandpa by Robert Kimmell Smith

Wemberley Worried by Kevin Henkes

When I Was Five by Arthur Howard

Text to text

Fireflies by Julie Brinckloe and *Fireflies for Nathan* by Ruth Oppenheim

Julie of the Wolves by Jean Craighead George and *Island of the Blue Dolphins* by Scott O'Dell

Lily's Purple Plastic Purse by Kevin Henkes and **Chester's Way** by Kevin Henkes

My Rotten Red-Headed Older Brother by Patricia Polacco and **My Ol' Man** by Patricia Polacco

Stellaluna by Janell Cannon and **Goose** by Molly Bang

Up North at the Cabin by Marsha Wilson Chall and **Letter to the Lake** by Susan Swanson

Wemberley Worried by Kevin Henkes, *Lizzy and Skunk* by Marie-Louise Fitzpatrick, and **Thundercake** by Patricia Polacco

Text to world

Fly Away Home by Eve Bunting

The Memory Box by Mary Bahr

Smoky Night by Eve Bunting

The Wednesday Surprise by Eve Bunting

Wilfrid Gordon McDonald Partridge by Mem Fox

Questioning

Bonaparte by Marsha Wilson Chall

Dr. White by Jane Goodall

Island of the Blue Dolphins by Scott O'Dell

Knots on a Counting Rope by Bill Martin

Mr. Mumble by Peter Catalanotto

The Patchwork Quilt by Valerie Fluornoy

Stone Fox by John Reynolds Gardiner

Tar Beach by Faith Ringgold

Through Grandpa's Eyes by Patricia MacLachlan

Tuck Everlasting by Natalie Babbitt

The Wall by Eve Bunting

Widget by Lyn Rossiter McFarland

Visualizing

All the Places to Love by Patricia MacLachlan

Charlotte's Web by E. B. White

Fireflies by Julie Brinckloe

Grandpa's Face by Eloise Greenfield

Harriet by Deborah Inkpen

I Love You the Purplest by Barbara M. Joosse

Silver Morning by Susan Pearson

Snail's Spell by Joanne Ryder

Stone Fox by John Reynolds Gardiner

The Storm Book by Charlotte Zolotow

Making Inferences

Annie and the Old One by Miska Miles

Bedtime for Frances by Russell Hoban

Dear Willie Rudd by Libba Moore Gray

The Leaving Morning by Angela Johnston

More Than Anything Else by Marie Bradby

Tar Beach by Faith Ringgold

Teammates by Peter Golenbock

The Wednesday Surprise by Eve Bunting

When Jessie Came Across the Sea by Amy Hest

Making It Your Own

An Angel for Solomon Singer by Cynthia Rylant

Eleanor by Barbara Cooney

Emily by Michael Bedard

Finding the Titanic by Robert D. Ballard

The Gardener by Sarah Stewart

Hawk Hill by Suzie Gilbert

Interrupted Journey by Kathryn Lasky

The Keeping Quilt by Patricia Polacco

The Other Side by Jacqueline Woodson

Seven Blind Mice by Ed Young

Sky Dancer by Jack Bushnell

Turtle, Turtle, Watch Out! by April Pulley Sayre

The Wednesday Surprise by Eve Bunting

Looking Back

Be Good to Eddie Lee by Virginia Fleming

Bridge to Terabithia by Katherine Paterson

The Keeping Quilt by Patricia Polacco

Letters from Rifka by Karen Hesse

Number the Stars by Lois Lowry

DAY 2: READ ALOUD AND SCRIPT OF THE MINI-LESSON

The next day Marybeth brought in a teddy bear. She used the bear to introduce the book *Lizzy and Skunk* by Marie-Louise Fitzpatrick. In this book Lizzy has a puppet named Skunk. Lizzy is afraid of many things, but appears braver when she has Skunk. However, one day she loses Skunk, and she must now be the brave one as she searches for him. In reading this book, Marybeth not only wanted the students to make connections from the text to their own lives but wanted to show them how they can make connections from one text to another.

Teacher: *I'd like you to meet someone. This is my teddy bear, Sufie. He's very old. This one's not his real eye. My mom had to replace it. I rubbed him just like Wemberley in the*

book *Wemberley Worried* rubbed her rabbit's ears. Sufie is really worn. My mom repaired his bottom. I wanted you to meet my bear, Sufie, because I'm going to talk about how books can remind you of your own life. Thinking of your own life can help you understand the book better. Today I'm going to read *Lizzy and Skunk*. I want you to use what you already know in your head. Also, remember the book we read yesterday about Wemberley. Now, look at the cover of this book. Which one is Lizzy and which one is Skunk?

Student: The little girl is Lizzy.

(Marybeth begins to read the book.)

T: I notice this little girl likes to talk to Skunk, her stuffed animal. When I was little, we had good conversations—just me and my bear.

S: What kind of conversations?

T: Like what we were going to have for dinner.

T: I remember needing a night light when I was little, but when Sufie was with me I didn't need it. Sufie was brave.

(Marybeth continues reading the book. The following conversation takes place during the read aloud.)

T: Does this book remind you of anything in *Wemberley Worried*?

S: She had lots of worries.

T: Yes, Wemberley did have a lot of worries. This book reminds me of myself <u>and</u> the other book we read.

T: What did the author do with Skunk that surprised you?

S: Skunk was scared.

T: You're right. Skunk is scared. But Lizzy always thought Skunk was brave for her.

T: It looks like Lizzy has lost Skunk. Can you remember a time when you lost something very important?

S: I lost my bike.

S: I lost my dad's watch. But then we found it.

T: How does the author let you know what happened to Skunk?

S: The picture shows us the cat took Skunk.

T: Does Lizzy know what happened to her skunk?

S: No.

T: Why not?

S: She didn't see the cat.

T: Lizzy is going to places now, but not with Skunk. She's getting brave. Was she very brave? Did she do it all by herself?

S: Yes.

T: How was that different from the very beginning of the book?

S: In the beginning Lizzy was scared and needed Skunk with her.

T: Who was scared at the end of the book?

S: Skunk was.

T: Who was brave at the end?

S: Lizzy was.

T: How do you think Skunk helped Lizzy?

S: Lizzy had to be brave and do things she didn't before so she could find Skunk.

T: When I read this book I thought about my bear, because I thought of my own life. I thought about how I needed my Sufie. Good readers always are thinking of how books remind them of their own life. So today in reading, think of how your books remind you of things so you can make connections between your reading and your life.

FOLLOW UP

The following week, we read the book *Thunder Cake* by Patricia Polacco to continue our work on having students make connections between themselves and the text and from one text to another. Barbara chose this book because she used to live in the area where the author grew up—the setting of many of her books. Barbara was able to show students how she made connections to the setting in this book. She also showed them connections she made to the character's fear of thunderstorms with her own sister's fear of storms. While reading the book, a student pointed out that the book reminded her of both Wemberley and Lizzy, the characters from the books the previous week, because they were scared of things, too. This is exactly what we want our students to do. As we model our lesson, we want students to see the connections we make and then continue to make more connections themselves.

Eight Key Reading Strategy Lesson Plans

In this section we elaborate on key reading strategies (those asterisked in the list on page 69). First, we present a brief explanation of each strategy, beginning the explanation with thoughts or questions our students have expressed when they've encountered the different strategies. We keep these phrases in mind because they help us to take "big ideas" and bring them down to our students' levels. This makes strategic reading more accessible to young readers.

Next we present lesson plans for each of the eight strategies. Let these plans guide you as you get started. We believe that the mini-lessons on reading strategies are the most important lessons you will teach. They are lessons that you will return to over and over again. By helping your students become strategic readers, you will assist them in becoming life-long readers.

Looking Ahead

> "I already know a little about…"
> "I think this book is going to be about…"

Most readers use this strategy, which we call "Looking Ahead," when beginning a new text. A reader draws on background knowledge and brings some personal experiences to his or her reading. For example, before proficient readers even begin *Stellaluna* by Janell Cannon, they think about the title of the book and decide if the cover is appealing. They consider what they already know about the topic and if they've read books by this author. Their personal experiences play a big role in understanding what they read. And because the experiences are specific to an individual and define what he or she brings to the text, each reader approaches a book from a unique context.

Fix-Up Strategies

> *"I think I'd better reread this…."*
> *"I'm confused about…."*

Proficient readers know when their reading doesn't make sense. When they are confused by a passage or vocabulary, they deal with the problem <u>as</u> they encounter it in the text. They use fix-up strategies such as rereading, reading on, and adjusting their pace. They know when to use context clues or decoding strategies and when to ask for help. Less able readers usually aren't aware when they are having difficulty. And they don't know how to remedy the situation. They need our help as they encounter difficulty. The teacher needs to show these readers strategies to use when something doesn't sound right or make sense.

Making Connections

> *"That reminds me of…"*

Proficient readers use prior knowledge, information, and experiences to make meaning from text. They search for connections between what they know and new information they encounter in their reading. They may make connections between a book and their own life. They may make connections between two or more books. Or they may make connections between a book and real-world knowledge and events.

Consider the following three types of connections (Keene & Zimmerman, 1997):

Text to Self: In this type of connection, the student makes a personal connection between the book and himself. He may be reading the book *Canoe Days* by Gary Paulsen and be reminded of time spent canoeing at camp. Or the teacher may be reading *Fireflies* by Julie Brinckloe, and it might remind students of hot summer evenings catching fireflies. A great book that just about anyone can identify with is *Gettin' Through Thursday* by Melrose Cooper. In this book a boy's celebration is put on hold until Friday, which is payday.

Text to Text: When readers make text-to-text connections, they are reading one book and thinking of similarities in another book or books they've read or had read to them. For example, while reading books by Patricia Polacco, readers may make connections among the characters or the settings in her books. Or they might make a connection from a theme in one of her books to a theme in a book by another author. After reading Polacco's *Thundercake,* and then listening to Marie-Louise Fitzpatrick's *Lizzy and Skunk,* one of our students made the connection that both books dealt with girls having fears. While reading aloud, you can model for young readers how to make comparisons among books and stories.

Text to World: This third way of making connections refers to a reader's linking real-world knowledge—perhaps that rainforests are in danger or that penguins live in the South Pole and not the North Pole—with what he or she is reading. While choosing books to introduce to your students, keep aware of how themes in the books can be connected to societal concerns or issues. For example, when listening to a reading of *Wilfrid Gordon MacDonald Partridge* by Mem Fox or *The Memory Box* by Mary Bahr, students can discuss the care and concerns of the elderly, especially those residing in nursing homes or those suffering from Alzheimer's. Eve Bunting's books also offer excellent possibilities. Her book *Fly Away Home*, the story of a father and son living in an airport, lends itself to the issue of homelessness. *The Wednesday Surprise*, the story of a grandmother learning to read, deals with illiteracy.

Questioning

"I wonder…"

Experienced readers pose questions before, during, and after reading. They are able to assess what they already know and determine what they still need to know. Students who ask questions and search for answers monitor their comprehension as they construct meaning. Students who ask "Why is the book called *Tar Beach*?" are trying to make sense of the title. As students ask questions while listening to *Through Grandpa's Eyes* by Patricia MacLachlan, they are trying to interpret the dialogue between the grandfather and the grandson. Students who ask questions while reading *Mr. Mumble* by Peter Catalanotto are searching for meaning in what Mr. Mumble is saying. Informational texts constantly provide opportunities for readers to ask questions: "Why is the ocean salty?" "Where does the James River start?" "Why are some snakes born alive and others hatch from eggs?" Young children are always asking questions, but questioning should continue even as students mature in their reading.

Visualizing

"It's like a movie in my head.…"

Proficient readers visualize as they read, creating mind pictures to help them understand what they are reading. By visualizing, a reader personalizes the reading with a unique mental image. Consider the different images you get as you read *Silver Morning* by Susan Pearson and *The Storm Book* by Charlotte Zolotow. The strong use of nouns, verbs, and adjectives enhances your senses as you see (and almost smell) the barn in E. B. White's *Charlotte's Web*. An excellent book to read to students without showing them the illustrations is *Fireflies* by Julie Brinckloe. Most students have had experiences catching fireflies and can visualize catching them and putting them in a jar to take home.

Making Inferences

"I think the author is trying to say…"

Mature readers are able to read between the lines. They can determine a character's motivation and personality, identify themes, and draw conclusions. In other words, they are able to make inferences based on their particular background knowledge and experiences. As a result, understanding becomes personal and slightly varied from one reader to another. *Dear Willie Rudd* by Libba Moore Gray requires readers to make inferences based on clues the author gives about the setting's time and place. In addition, the reader can infer the feelings of the character and her reason for writing a letter to a deceased woman. In *Annie and the Old One* by Miska Miles, the reader can make inferences from the dialogue between Annie and her grandmother.

> ### TEACHER to TEACHER
> We have found that as we talk with younger students about inferences, they understand the concept better when we tell them it's like listening to the author's whispers. The author talks to the reader using the words and pictures of the story. However, the author leaves us clues, or whispers, as to those ideas that we need to infer for ourselves.

Making It Your Own

"I think I understand why..."

Experienced readers synthesize and summarize sections as they read. They determine the main idea and key points of the passage, or even develop a new perspective or way of thinking. In reading *The Other Side* by Jacqueline Woodson, many students may understand and articulate the author's message or identify the theme of the book. But the student who sees the fence dividing the black and white children, who connects the expression "sitting on the fence," and who verbalizes the unfairness, is synthesizing information from the text. Students who are able to synthesize are able to make generalizations and judgments as they consider their own personal feelings and attitudes on various issues.

A fifth grader keeps a response journal while reading.

Looking Back

"I need to share this book with someone...."
"My favorite part was when..."

Proficient readers take time when they are finished reading to reflect on what they have just read, especially when it is a particularly enjoyable book. They don't just close the book and put it away; they allow themselves time to linger over the pages. They seek out someone so they can discuss the book. They even allow time for reflection in their journal. After reading *Be Good to Eddie Lee* by Virginia Fleming, a fifth-grade class reflected on the two characters, one with Down Syndrome. The students were struck by how Eddie's knowledge and insight influenced the other child's actions. They stopped and paused. They needed to take a minute to reflect on what they had just read, to appreciate the language, and to ponder how they were affected by the book.

For proficient students, reading is something to savor, to value, to treasure. Strategic reading instruction helps all readers to develop this appreciation for reading.

On the next eight pages, we present a detailed lesson plan for each of the eight reading strategies described above. Our aim is to provide you with a model, a structure, and a set of recommendations based on what has worked for us. We hope you will find them useful as the basis for your own modifications and personalized lesson plans.

READING STRATEGY MINI-LESSON LESSON PLAN: LOOKING AHEAD

Rationale—Students need to know that their background knowledge and experiences will assist in their comprehending what they read.

Literature—*Stellaluna* (Cannon)

Materials—Bat puppet; pictures of bats; bird's nests

Connection—"Have you ever seen or heard a bat? What do you know about bats? We are going to use what you already know to help us understand this story better."

Purpose—"Today we are going to figure out what you already know before we even start reading. It will help us understand the story better."

Instruction—

Before
- ◆ Share title of book and show pictures on cover (if available).
- ◆ Determine prior knowledge or experiences that exist on the topic (e.g., bats).
- ◆ List on chart paper what you and the students already know.

During
- ◆ Read, stop, think aloud.
- ◆ Relate knowledge and personal experiences to the text.
- ◆ Model how personal knowledge or experience helps you understand the text.

After
- ◆ Add to the chart what has been learned.
- ◆ Determine if more information is needed to understand the passage better.
- ◆ State (with students' assistance) how to apply this strategy to their reading.

Questions for Discussion—
- ◆ How did our prior knowledge help us before we ever started reading?
- ◆ What similar experiences have you had that helped you understand the story?
- ◆ How does thinking about what you already know help you understand the passage better?
- ◆ What could you do if you are having difficulty understanding what you are reading?

Related Journal or Conference Focus—
- ◆ How did your prior knowledge help you understand the text?
- ◆ What experiences have you had that are similar to those in the book?
- ◆ Do you still have questions after reading the story or need more information on the topic?

Additional Literature to Use for Strategy Reinforcement

Finding the Titanic (Ballard)

Fireflies (Brinckloe)

The Raft (LeMarche)

Verdi (Cannon)

When I Was Young in the Mountains (Rylant)

Nonfiction books

READING STRATEGY MINI-LESSON LESSON PLAN: USING FIX-UP STRATEGIES

Rationale—Students need to know a variety of strategies that they can rely on when they are having difficulty understanding text.

Literature—*Dory Story* (Pallotta)

Materials—Thinking cap; serious-looking glasses

Connection—"We have talked about what to do when you have trouble figuring out a word. Today we are going to talk about what to do when you are confused in your reading or if something doesn't make sense."

Purpose—"Today I am going to show you what I call 'fix-up strategies.' These strategies will help you when you come to a word that you're not sure of. They will also help you if you are confused and you need to do some re-reading."

Instruction—

Before
- Share title and cover of book.
- Preview book, passage, or chapter.
- Determine prior knowledge or experiences.

During
- Read, stop, think aloud.
- Demonstrate what you do when you come to an unfamiliar word (look for a chunk in the word, use context or syntax clues, read ahead, slow down).
- Demonstrate how you reread to clarify a confusing part.
- Model how you adjust your rate of reading to assist in understanding a difficult passage.

After
- Review what "fix-up" strategies were utilized and for what purpose.
- Determine if other strategies are needed to understand the passage better.
- State (with students' assistance) how to apply "fix-up" strategies to their reading.
- Determine level of understanding. What still needs to be done?

Questions for Discussion—
- What did we do when we came to an unfamiliar word?
- What did we do when we came to a confusing passage?
- Why is it necessary to adjust our rate of reading? When should we slow down/speed up?
- What will you do when you are having difficulty understanding what you are reading?

Related Journal or Conference Focus—
- What problems did you have while reading your story/text?
- How did using a "fix-up" strategy help you understand the passage better?
- What do you understand now that you didn't understand before?

Additional Literature to Use for Strategy Reinforcement

Big books

Chapter books (*Shiloh, Tuck Everlasting, Bridge to Terabithia*)

Nonfiction books (*Top of the World: Climbing Mt. Everest*)

READING STRATEGY MINI-LESSON LESSON PLAN:
MAKING CONNECTIONS—TEXT TO TEXT

Rationale—Students need to know how we make connections between books. It may be that they are by the same author, have similar characters, setting, events, or themes.

Literature—*My Ol'Man* (Polacco)   *My Rotten Redheaded Older Brother* (Polacco)

Materials—A collection of several books by the same author

Connection—"Today I am going to show you how reading one book makes me think of other books."

Purpose—"Today I want you to pay attention to what I do as I read. I am going to stop when I am reminded of something in another book."

Instruction—

Before ◆ Share title of book and show pictures on cover (if available).
◆ Preview book, passage, or chapter.
◆ Determine similar characters, setting, events, and familiarity of author.

During ◆ Read, stop, think aloud.
◆ Relate knowledge and personal experiences to the text.
◆ Show how this book is similar to others you have read.
◆ Relate how the character's attributes are similar to other characters you've read about, or to other characters in books by the same author.
◆ Show how this book takes place in a setting similar to another book.
◆ Identify familiar themes in the book.
◆ Show how the writing style is similar to another familiar book.
◆ Show how making connections can aid in understanding.

After ◆ Make connections from the story to other books—compare setting, feelings, events, theme.

Questions for Discussion—

◆ How did previous reading experiences help us make connections to this book?
◆ What books have you read that helped you make connections to this book?
◆ What different kinds of connections were you able to make to other books?

Related Journal or Conference Focus—

◆ What connections to other books did you make as you read?
◆ What similar characteristics did you see in books by the same author?

Additional Literature to Use for Strategy Reinforcement

Fireflies (Brinckloe) and *Fireflies for Nathan* (Oppenheim)

Julie of the Wolves (George) and *Island of the Blue Dolphins* (O'Dell)

Lily's Purple Plastic Purse (Henkes) and *Chester's Way* (Henkes)

Stellaluna (Cannon) and *Goose* (Bang)

Up North at the Cabin (Chall) and *Letter to the Lake* (Swanson)

READING STRATEGY MINI-LESSON LESSON PLAN: QUESTIONING

Rationale—Students need to know that they should be asking questions of themselves while they read. Sometimes they only do it before they start reading.

Literature—*Tar Beach* (Ringgold)

Materials—Tar or tar paper (if available) or picture of men working on road with hot tar to clarify the nature and role of city rooftops; sticky notes

Connection—"Good readers are constantly asking themselves questions while they read. Do you remember when I did that yesterday?"

Purpose—"When I read today I want you to notice when I stop and ask myself questions. I might do that when I come to a new word or when I'm confused."

Instruction—

Before ◆ Share title and cover of book. See if students know what tar is.

◆ Ask questions before you begin reading to generate enthusiasm.

◆ Explain that you will read the book and stop and ask yourself questions as you go along.

During ◆ Read, stop, and ask a question; think aloud how you are getting the answer: using prior knowledge and experiences, hints from the text, other resources.

◆ Demonstrate how asking questions as you read provides reason to continue reading.

◆ Show how you can use sticky notes to mark places where you have questions.

After ◆ Determine if your questions still exist.

◆ Look at sticky notes to see if questions were answered yet.

◆ State (with students' assistance) how to apply this strategy to their reading.

Questions for Discussion—
◆ What questions did you have <u>before</u> you began reading?
◆ What questions did you have <u>while</u> you were reading?
◆ How did stopping and asking yourself a question help you understand the passage better?
◆ How could using a sticky note help you when you have a question while reading?

Related Journal or Conference Focus—
◆ What questions did you have while reading?
◆ How did your personal knowledge help you answer your questions?
◆ How did the text or pictures help you answer your questions?
◆ How did the use of sticky notes help you with your questions?

Additional Literature to Use for Strategy Reinforcement

Island of the Blue Dolphins (O'Dell)

The Patchwork Quilt (Flournoy)

Mr. Mumble (Catalanotto)

Stone Fox (Gardiner)

Through Grandpa's Eyes (MacLachlan)

Tuck Everlasting (Babbitt)

Revisiting the Reading Workshop: Management, Mini-Lessons, and Strategies • Scholastic Professional Books

READING STRATEGY MINI-LESSON LESSON PLAN: VISUALIZING

Rationale—Students need to know that they should be visualizing as they read. As students move into books without pictures, they must create their own images.

Literature—*Fireflies* (Brinckloe)

Materials—Cover for book jacket so illustrations are not seen; large glass jar with holes in the lid

Connection—"Yesterday we talked about how illustrators help us get a picture of the story in our head. Today you are going to just listen to a story and use the author's descriptions to create a picture in your head."

Purpose—"When I read today, I want you to think about the movie you are seeing in your head. How is the author helping you create those pictures?"

Instruction—

Before ◈ Share title and cover of book.

◈ Determine knowledge of catching fireflies (lightning bugs).

◈ Explain that you will read the book without showing the illustrations.

During ◈ Read, stop, think aloud.

◈ Model how you close your eyes and get an image based on the author's words or your prior knowledge.

◈ Have students close their eyes and get an image.

◈ Demonstrate images interpreted from text (e.g. opening jar to release fireflies).

After ◈ Share images with one another.

◈ Compare to illustrations in book (if available).

◈ State (with students' assistance) how to apply this strategy to their reading.

Questions for Discussion—

◈ What did you "see" when I read _____?

◈ What details in the story helped you see the characters/the setting?

◈ What did the author do to create images for you?

◈ What similar experiences have you had that helped you get a picture in your mind?

◈ How does visualizing what you are reading help you understand the passage better?

Related Journal or Conference Focus—

◈ Describe images you were able to create while reading.

◈ How did your images differ from the illustrations in the book?

◈ How did illustrations in your book help you with your images?

◈ How did your images help you understand the story?

Additional Literature to Use for Strategy Reinforcement

All the Places to Love (MacLachlan)

Charlotte's Web (White)

I Love You the Purplest (Joosse)

Silver Morning (Pearson)

Snail's Spell (Ryder)

The Storm Book (Zolotow)

READING STRATEGY MINI-LESSON LESSON PLAN: MAKING INFERENCES

Rationale—Students need to be able to use the information in the text as well as their own prior knowledge to infer meaning.

Literature—*Dear Willie Rudd* (Gray)

Materials—Attractive stationery with envelope to introduce the letter writing format of the book; magnifying glass to act like a detective

Connection—"We have been talking about how we use our own knowledge or prior experiences to make sense of our reading. Today we are going to use that knowledge and any clues in the text to figure out what the author is telling us."

Purpose—"When we read today, I want you to be detectives. Sometimes the authors don't give you all the information. You must 'read between the lines' to figure things out."

Instruction—

Before ◆ "Why do you think the author made the title sound like she was writing a letter?"
◆ Explain that authors don't tell the reader everything. Sometimes the reader must figure out what the author is saying. This can be done based on what you know or hints in the text. Act like a detective and "read between the lines."

During ◆ Read, stop, think aloud.
◆ Demonstrate how you are inferring meaning:
from prior knowledge: setting in the south because of magnolia trees.
from information in the text: worked as a maid because of the apron and scrubbed floors.

After ◆ Discuss parts in the story where inferences were made.
◆ Where could you use your prior knowledge or personal experiences?
◆ When did you need to rely on the text for help?

Questions for Discussion—
◆ What did the author do to help you understand the character and her actions (e.g. Why this woman needed to write to Willie Rudd)?
◆ What prior knowledge or personal experiences have you had that helped you figure out this story?
◆ How can making inferences help you understand and personalize a story?
◆ How can two readers using their personal experiences infer slightly different meanings?

Related Journal or Conference Focus—
◆ What clues did the author give you to help you figure out a passage?
◆ How did making an inference help you understand the passage better?
◆ How did your own personal experiences help you understand what you were reading?

Additional Literature to Use for Strategy Reinforcement
Annie and the Old One (Miles)   *Tar Beach* (Ringgold)

The Leaving Morning (Johnston)   *The Wednesday Surprise* (Bunting)

More Than Anything Else (Bradby)   *When Jessie Came Across the Sea* (Hest)

READING STRATEGY MINI-LESSON LESSON PLAN: MAKING IT YOUR OWN

Rationale—Students need to know how to reflect on their reading, to be able to summarize and synthesize what they've read.

Literature—*The Other Side* (Woodson)

Materials—Journal; sticky notes

Connection—"Readers do a lot of thinking while they read. I want you to be able to see me think about my reading."

Purpose—"I am going to show you what I do when I think about what I am reading. I will show you how I stop, pause, and reflect. Sometimes I will write a note down in my journal, sometimes I will use a sticky note, and sometimes I will just stop and quietly think."

Instruction—

Before ◈ Preview book before reading to determine purpose.
◈ Determine knowledge of subject.
◈ Explain that you will read the book and then reflect, take notes in a journal, and use sticky notes.

During ◈ Read; pause to reflect; verbalize what was read by restating in your own words.
◈ Take notes in a journal of key points and events.
◈ Mark passages to remember with sticky notes.
◈ Reread parts to remember.
◈ Adjust rate of reading.

After ◈ Share notes in journal or passages marked with sticky notes.
◈ Use the notes to summarize verbally what was read.
◈ Model writing a summary on the passage read using a journal and/or sticky notes (include a topic sentence and detail sentences).
◈ Show how your summary can include conclusions, judgments, new ideas, or thoughts you have drawn from your reading.

Questions for Discussion—

◈ How does pausing to reflect and restating in your own words help you to summarize?
◈ If you had to summarize what you read in just a few sentences, what would you say?
◈ What has the author made you think differently about?
◈ What conclusions or judgments have you made after this reading?

Related Journal or Conference Focus—

◈ Use your notes to summarize what you read.
◈ How did using sticky notes to mark parts to remember help in writing a summary?
◈ How did pausing and reflecting on what you had read help you personalize your reading?

Additional Literature to Use for Strategy Reinforcement

Bridge to Terabithia (Paterson)   *Sky Dancer* (Bushnell)
Hawk Hill (Gilbert)   *Turtle, Turtle, Watch Out!* (Sayre)
Interrupted Journey (Lasky)   *The Wednesday Surprise* (Bunting)

READING STRATEGY MINI-LESSON LESSON PLAN: LOOKING BACK

Rationale—Students need to know how to reflect on their reading, to appreciate the reading experience they just had.

Literature—*Be Good to Eddie Lee* (Fleming)

Materials—Journal; sticky notes; telephone

Connection—"Readers do a lot of thinking and reflecting after they have finished reading. I want to show you what I do when I finish a book."

Purpose—"Today I am going to show you what I do when I finish reading something. I will show you how I stop and reflect. Sometimes I will write a note down in my journal. This is especially important if I want to remember this book for something in the future. Sometimes I will call my sister and tell her about this great book I read. We share titles all the time. And sometimes I will just stop and quietly think about the book."

Instruction—

During
◆ Read; pause to reflect on reading; verbalize what is having an impact.
◆ Take notes in a journal.
◆ Mark passages to remember with sticky notes.
◆ Reread parts to remember.
◆ Adjust rate of reading.

After
◆ Model the sort of entry to write in a journal after completing it.
◆ Model sharing the book with a sibling or a friend by using the phone.

Questions for Discussion—
◆ How does reflecting help you appreciate and savor the reading?
◆ If you had to share with others an incredible book, what would you say?
◆ What has the author done to make you feel so strongly about this book?
◆ What conclusions or judgments have you made after this reading?

Related Journal or Conference Focus—
◆ Use your notes to help you reflect on what you read.
◆ How did using sticky notes to mark parts to remember help you in reflecting on your reading?
◆ How did pausing and reflecting on what you had read help you personalize your reading?

Additional Literature to Use for Strategy Reinforcement

Bridge to Terabithia (Paterson)   *Number the Stars* (Lowry)

The Keeping Quilt (Polacco)   *The Other Side* (Woodson)

Letters from Rifka (Hesse)   Personal books from home for sharing

Miss Rumphius (Cooney)

Developing Mini-Lessons on Reading Skills

Reading skills also play a key role in helping students understand text. To be successful, readers must develop a repertoire of fundamental reading skills—skills that will enable them to do everything from grasp the main idea to understand the sequence or interpret a diagram within a reading selection.

Topics for Mini-Lessons on Reading Skills

A detailed list of possible topics for mini-lessons on reading skills is just below. These are all skills that you'll want your students to use regularly and automatically as they read.

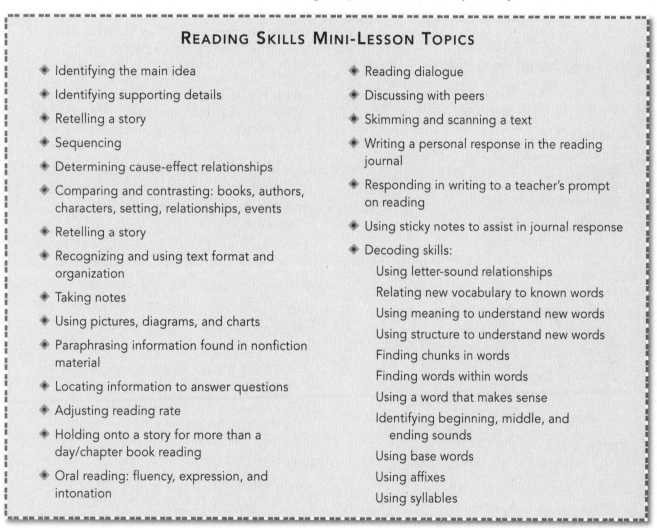

READING SKILLS MINI-LESSON TOPICS

- Identifying the main idea
- Identifying supporting details
- Retelling a story
- Sequencing
- Determining cause-effect relationships
- Comparing and contrasting: books, authors, characters, setting, relationships, events
- Retelling a story
- Recognizing and using text format and organization
- Taking notes
- Using pictures, diagrams, and charts
- Paraphrasing information found in nonfiction material
- Locating information to answer questions
- Adjusting reading rate
- Holding onto a story for more than a day/chapter book reading
- Oral reading: fluency, expression, and intonation

- Reading dialogue
- Discussing with peers
- Skimming and scanning a text
- Writing a personal response in the reading journal
- Responding in writing to a teacher's prompt on reading
- Using sticky notes to assist in journal response
- Decoding skills:
    Using letter-sound relationships
    Relating new vocabulary to known words
    Using meaning to understand new words
    Using structure to understand new words
    Finding chunks in words
    Finding words within words
    Using a word that makes sense
    Identifying beginning, middle, and ending sounds
    Using base words
    Using affixes
    Using syllables

Recommended Books for Mini-Lessons on Reading Skills

If you have not previously used literature to teach reading skills, the lists on page 86 will help you get started. For example, a wonderful way to teach your students how to compare settings is to have them read *When I Was Young in the Mountains* and *Amber on the Mountain*. When your students are familiar with these titles, have them compare the events in *Amber on the Mountain* to those in *More Than Anything Else*. Because the students are putting to use the concepts of compare and contrast within books they really care about understanding, they learn these skills more thoroughly than they would if they were just asked to complete worksheets.

As with our earlier list on books for teaching reading strategies, this is an extensive—but by no means exhaustive—list of books for some of the strategies listed on p. 85.

RECOMMENDED BOOKS FOR TEACHING SKILLS MINI-LESSONS

Identifying the Main Idea

Great Kapok Tree by Lynne Cherry

The Keeping Quilt by Patricia Polacco

Miss Rumphius by Barbara Cooney

Mufaro's Beautiful Daughters by John Steptoe

Reason for a Flower by Ruth Heller

Stellaluna by Janell Cannon

Identifying Supporting Details

Chickens Aren't the Only Ones by Ruth Heller

An Octopus Is Amazing by Patricia Lauber

Retelling a Story

Fireflies by Julie Brinckloe

The Hickory Chair by Lisa Rose Fraustino

Ira Sleeps Over by Bernard Waber

Owl Babies by Martin Waddell

Sick Day by Patricia MacLachlan

When Jessie Came Across the Sea by Amy Hest

Sequencing

Hot-Air Henry by Mary Calhoun

The Mitten by Jan Brett

Ox-Cart Man by Donald Hall

Pancakes, Pancakes by Eric Carle

Stone Soup by Marcia Brown

Turnip by Pierr Morgan

Identifying Cause and Effect

The Gingerbread Boy by Paul Galdone

The Mitten by Jan Brett

Pig and Crow by Kay Chorao

The Tiny Seed by Eric Carle

Why I Will Never, Ever, Ever, Ever Have Enough Time to Read This Book by Remy Charlip

Comparing and Contrasting

Texts

Bookshop Dog and *Cookie Store Cat* by Cynthia Rylant

Dear Mr. Blueberry by Simon James and *Nice Try Tooth Fairy* by Mary W. Olson

Lost by Paul Brett Johnson and Celeste Lewis and *The Snow Lambs* by Debi Gliori

Characters

Cinderella by Charles Perrault, *The Rough Face Girl* by Rafe Martin, *Egyptian Cinderella* by Shirley Climo, and *Princess Furball* by Anita Lobel

Jack and the Beanstalk by Steven Kellogg and *Jim and the Beanstalk* by Raymond Briggs

Stellaluna by Janell Cannon and *Goose* by Molly Bang

The Three Little Pigs by James Marshall and *The Three Javelinas* by Susan Lowell

Setting

City Mouse and Country Mouse by Aesop

Tar Beach by Faith Ringgold and *Smoky Night* by Eve Bunting

Train to Somewhere by Eve Bunting and *When Jessie Came Across the Sea* by Amy Hest

When I Was Young in the Mountains by Cynthia Rylant and *Amber on the Mountain* by Tony Johnston

Events

Amber on the Mountain by Tony Johnston and *More Than Anything Else* by Marie Bradby

Wemberley Worried by Kevin Henkes and *Lizzy and Skunk* by Marie-Louise Fitzpatrick

When Jessie Came Across the Sea by Amy Hest and *Watch the Stars Come Out* by Riki Levinson

Extended Sample Reading Skill Mini-Lesson

While working with a group of first graders, we decided to focus on the skill of getting the students to retell a story in their own words. Retelling provides helpful information on students' level of understanding. We chose to teach a mini-lesson on this topic because we wanted our students to know how to retell a story during their individual reading conferences.

Retelling a Story

Marybeth begins her lesson by asking, "Are you sitting next to someone you can 'think' next to?" She wants to make sure the students are displaying good listening behavior. She then says, "Tell me what we have been talking about in our Reading Workshop read alouds." She is helping students connect today's lesson with previous lessons.

Student: the parts of the story.

Teacher: You're right. And these parts of the story, or story elements, help us understand it. They are also going to help us retell the story. Today after I read, we are going to think about the beginning, middle, and end of the story so we can retell it—put the story in our own words so that we can tell it to someone else. Let's try it.

Today I am going to read *Owl Babies*. Let's look at this picture and see if you can get an idea of the setting of the story. The illustrator gives us a clue of the setting. What do you see?

S: It's in the woods at night.

T: That's what it looks like. Let's read and check it out.

(Teacher begins to read book.)

T: You are correct. The setting is in a forest.

(Teacher continues.)

T: Do you detect a problem in our story?

S: Their mommy is gone.

T: And how are they feeling?

S: Sad.

S: Lonely.

T: How would you feel if your mommy was gone?

S: Scared.

T: You're all right. I think they are having all those feelings.

(Teacher continues.)

T: Why does Sarah want all of them to sit on her branch?

S: Because she wants them to wait with her.

T: Yes, I think she wants some company because she's scared.

(Teacher continues.)

T: I see a solution to the problem.

S: The mommy is coming back.

S: They won't be scared now.

S: The last page said almost the same thing as the other pages but instead of saying "I want my mommy," Bill says, "I love my mommy."

T: Talk with me about the story elements. Who were the characters?

S: The three owls.

T: Just the three owls?

S: Oh, and the mom, too.

T: Okay, we know the setting and the characters. What was the problem in the story?

S: Their mommy was gone.

T: That is a problem. Now let's talk about the beginning, middle, and ending—the events in the story. What was one of the events in the beginning?

S: Their mommy left.

T: That happened real early in the book. What did the owls do through the whole middle of the book?

S: Bill only said, "I want my mommy."

T: Well, what did Sarah do?

S: Sarah tried to be brave.

T: She did try to be the brave one. Did the owls do anything or go anywhere?

S: They just talked and stayed together.

T: What about the end?

S: The mommy came home.

S: And Bill said, "I love my mommy."

T: You did a really important reading job. You retold the story of *Owl Babies*. When you are able to retell the story, it helps you understand the story. Readers need to think what happened in the whole story—in the beginning, in the middle, and at the end. Good readers use what's going on in their head to help them retell a story. Today in your book nook when you are finished reading a book, I want you to do what we did together. Think about the beginning, middle, and ending of the story. I'm going to ask you to retell your story when I come to your book nook for a conference. Let's get started.

Later, at share time, Marybeth invites several students to share their retellings. After the retellings, Marybeth asks students to notice what each of the children did. She points out that they didn't need to look at their books or to look at the pictures. They were able to remember the story and to use the knowledge that was already in their minds—skills that good readers possess.

CHAPTER 6

Exploring the Text:

Mini-Lessons on Literary Elements and Literary Techniques

"Remember when we read *Knots on a Counting Rope*, and we saw that different text format? My book today has a different text format too."
—Devonte, grade 2

The borders between reading and writing are very fuzzy. As a result, good readers are usually successful writers. They read across various genres and from a variety of authors. They can recognize a writer's style, the author's point of view, and figurative language. Typically, because their reading experiences are simpler and more limited, less able readers do not have the same exposure to literacy conventions. The teacher's job is to provide rich literature experiences for all students. You can do this through read alouds, by deliberately exposing students to various genres, by introducing them to new authors, and by sharing the language of books. When your students are able to "read like writers" and to "write like readers," you know you have been successful as a literacy teacher. Mini-lessons on literary elements and techniques can assist them.

Literary Elements and Literary Techniques Instruction

When you teach literary <u>elements</u>, your focus is on characters, setting, plot, and theme. Literary <u>techniques</u> include what an author does to craft his or her work. Through the use of symbolism, mood, and figurative language, an author develops a unique style. Involving students in mini-lessons on literary elements and techniques gives them a voice to communicate as well as an ability to analyze literature. Their knowledge of the story elements, the structure of text, and the author's craft and techniques is invaluable. You will find that it strengthens their understanding of what they read and enlivens their own writing.

Mini-lessons on literary elements enable your students to analyze a text. Students need to:

- 📖 become familiar with the different genres and to recognize the elements of literature.

- 📖 identify the character's attributes and growth as well as the importance of the setting in the story.

- 📖 recognize the organization of the story and to see how the author developed the plot.

- 📖 understand how reading nonfiction differs from reading fiction.

- 📖 identify and use the characteristics of nonfiction to assist them in obtaining meaning from the text.

Mini-lessons on literary techniques call your students' attention to the author's use of language. In this way, these lessons lend themselves nicely to the Writing Workshop, as well as to the Reading Workshop. With the connections between their reading and their writing in mind, students can more easily learn how to improve their writing by developing their own techniques or craft. For example:

- 📖 By recognizing how an author showed a character's change over time, a student can incorporate this technique into his or her own story.

- 📖 By focusing on the author's use of dialogue, a student can see its role in his own story.

These mini-lessons also provide you with the perfect opportunity to teach punctuating and formatting paragraphs with dialogue.

Developing Mini-Lessons on Literary Elements

Good readers go beyond the literal interpretation of the text. They form a sense of the setting, visualize the characters' actions, and anticipate the ending to the story. Good authors allow us to get lost in their books and to appreciate their use of language. We laugh at Max in *Bunny Money* (Wells), cheer on the ducklings in *Make Way for Ducklings* (McCloskey), whisper when we read *Owl Moon* (Yolen), and cry when Little Ann joins Old Dan at the end in *Where the Red Fern Grows* (Rawls). By targeting the key literary elements for instruction within the context of good literature, you are giving your students a great boost toward creative, proficient reading and writing.

Topics for Mini-Lessons on Literary Elements

The list below gives you some examples of possible mini-lessons on literary elements. Use it in conjunction with the list of recommended books that follows as you plan your Reading Workshop mini-lessons.

> ### TEACHER to TEACHER
> A great book for teaching the problem, events, and resolution to intermediate students is *The Bear That Heard Crying*. It is based on a real-life event in 1783 where a three-year-old girl was lost in the woods. Teachers like this book because it is a picture book with longer text and an engaging story line.

TOPICS FOR MINI-LESSONS ON LITERARY ELEMENTS

- Author's choice of a book title
- Characters:
    - Relating the character(s) to the setting
    - Character's development and change over time
    - Determining the main character and secondary characters
- Setting:
    - Time and place
    - Importance of the setting to the story
- Theme of the book
- Mood or tone
- Passage of time in the book
- Change over time:
    - Effect on the setting
    - Effect on the characters
- Identifying story language
- Story patterns:
    - Identifying the beginning, middle, and ending

- Identifying the problem, central idea, events, and resolution
- Identifying the story shape: linear, circular
- Use of story maps or graphic organizers
- Recognizing the lead
- Recognizing the conclusion
- Function and terminology of parts of the book
- The difference in fiction versus nonfiction
- Different role of illustrations in fiction versus nonfiction
- Narration of the story/point of view—how it affects the reader
- Genre:
    - Identification of category
    - Characteristics of category
- Author's purpose
- Use of dialogue: Is it realistic?
- Author and/or illustrator studies

Recommended Books for Mini-Lessons on Literary Elements

As in the previous chapter, we include here a list of some of our favorite books to teach some of the literary elements and techniques. While these books are appropriate for most grade levels, the more challenging titles or chapter books are indicated in boldface within certain categories.

RECOMMENDED BOOKS FOR LITERARY ELEMENTS MINI-LESSONS

Relating Characters to the Setting

Amber on the Mountain by Tony Johnston

Come a Tide by George Ella Lyon

Hatchet by Gary Paulsen

Legend of the Loon by Kathy-Jo Wargin

Miss Rumphius by Barbara Cooney

On Call Back Mountain by Eve Bunting

Tar Beach by Faith Ringgold

Up North at the Cabin by Marsha Wilson Chall

Where the Red Fern Grows by Wilson Rawls

Character's Development and Change Over Time

Amazing Grace by Mary Hoffman

Amber on the Mountain by Tony Johnston

Chrysanthemum by Kevin Henkes

Island of the Blue Dolphins by Scott O'Dell

Julie of the Wolves by Jean Craighead George

Noisy Nora by Rosemary Wells

The Pinballs by Betsy Byars

The Raft by Jim LaMarche

Ramona Forever by Beverly Cleary

Rolling Rose by James Stevenson

Sign of the Beaver by Elizabeth George Speare

Stone Fox by John Russell Gardiner

Train to Somewhere by Eve Bunting

Theme

The Eagle and the Wren by Jane Goodall

Koala Lou by Mem Fox

Stellaluna by Janell Cannon

The Ugly Duckling by Hans Christian Andersen

Wilfrid Gordon MacDonald Partridge by Mem Fox

Mood or Tone

Alexander and the Terrible, Horrible, No Good, Very Bad Day by Judith Viorst

Earrings! by Cynthia Rylant

Fly Away Home by Eve Bunting

The Leaving Morning by Angela Johnston

The Relatives Came by Cynthia Rylant

Sidewalk Story by Sharon Bell Mathis

Train to Somewhere by Eve Bunting

Passage of Time

Henry and Mudge: The First Book by Cynthia Rylant

The Hickory Chair by Lisa Rowe Fraustino

Miss Rumphius by Barbara Cooney

My Rotten Red Headed Older Brother by Patricia Polacco

The Raft by Jim LaMarche

When Jessie Came Across the Sea by Amy Hest

Story Patterns

Beginning, middle, ending

Fireflies by Julie Brinckloe

Owl Babies by Martin Waddell

The Relatives Came by Cynthia Rylant

Stellaluna by Janell Cannon

Thunder Cake by Patricia Polacco

Verdi by Jannell Cannon

Problem, solution, central idea

The Bear That Heard Crying by Natalie Kinsey-Warnock and Helen Kinsey

Fly Away Home by Eve Bunting

Grandpa's Too Good Garden by James Stevenson

Ming Lo Moves the Mountain by Arnold Lobel

The Wednesday Surprise by Eve Bunting

Story shape	Role of the Author/Illustrator
Circular:	Author sets of dePaola, Catalanotto, Polacco, Rylant, Stevens
If You Give a Mouse a Cookie by Laura Numeroff	
The Great Gracie Chase by Cynthia Rylant	**Role of Illustrations**
My Mama Had a Dancing Heart by Libba Moore Gray	*Carl* books by Alexandra Day
	Jumanji by Chris Van Allsburg
Watch the Stars Come Out by Riki Levinson	*Officer Buckle and Gloria* by Peggy Rathman
Linear:	*Rainbow Fish* by Marcus Pfister
Fireflies by Julie Brinckloe	Caldecott books
Max's Dragon Shirt by Rosemary Wells	Nonfiction books
Tops and Bottoms by Janet Stevens	Wordless books

Extended Sample Literary Elements Mini-Lesson

In this mini-lesson the teacher discusses the author's purpose with her students. Her focus is on their understanding and identifying the theme in a book. She chose the book *Koala Lou* (Fox) as the read aloud for this mini-lesson, because she believes many of her students will identify with not winning a race. *Koala Lou* is a good choice for a first lesson on the topic of "theme," because its theme is easily discernible.

IDENTIFYING THE THEME OF A BOOK

Teacher: We've been talking about the author's purpose for writing books. Some authors will write to give you information. A lot of the non-fiction books we read give us information. Other writers write to persuade you. We've looked at newspapers and how they try to give us their opinion and persuade us to feel a certain way. Some authors write to entertain us, to provide enjoyment as we read. We have read a lot of those kinds of books this year. I'm thinking of books like *Max's Dragon Shirt* and *The Relatives Came*. Those books are a lot of fun to read. But another thing that authors do is they often try to convey a message or a theme in their book.

Student: Like in the book *The Ugly Duckling*?

T: Yes, just like that. In that book, the Ugly Duckling wasn't accepted when he was younger because of his looks. But he grew up to be a beautiful swan. So the author's message or theme is that it doesn't matter what you look like but what you are like on the inside.

S: My mom says beauty is only skin deep.

T: Your mom is right. Well, today we are going to read a book that has a message or a theme. The book is called *Koala Lou*, and it is written by Mem Fox. We have read some of her other books this year. What do you already know about koalas?

S: They live in Australia.

T: Yes, you're right. And very few zoos in our country have koalas. Well, this book takes place in Australia since that is where the koalas live.

S: I think they have pouches like the kangaroos.

T: True. They are from the same family of animals called marsupials. We'll also see other animals in this book that live in Australia. Let me begin.

(Teacher begins to read the book.)

T: Do you notice how the author repeats the line: "Koala Lou, I DO love you!"?

S: That's probably an important part of the book.

T: Do you think it could be part of the author's message to the reader?

S: That the mom really loves her?

T: Let's see.

(Teacher continues reading.)

T: Koala Lou decides to enter the Bush Olympics. It's called the Bush Olympics because the bush is a forested area in Australia that doesn't have many people.

S: Weren't the Olympics in Australia last year?

T: You're right. They were. Let's continue to see how Koala Lou does.

S: I think she's going to win.

T: How do you think Koala Lou is feeling on the day of her event?

S: I bet she's nervous.

S: She's really nervous because Koala Klaws had a good climb.

T: Let's finish the book and see how Koala Lou does.

S: She's going to win.

(Teacher continues reading.)

T: How did Koala Lou feel after not winning, but coming in second?

S: She felt awful. It said she "cried her heart out."

T: I'm sure she was really disappointed. She wanted to win. We have all felt like Koala Lou at some time when we wanted to win but didn't come in first place.

S: That happens to me all the time.

T: And it's happened to me too. But let's think about Koala Lou and her mother. After Koala Lou came in second, her mother said: "Koala Lou, I DO love you! I always have, and I always will." It didn't matter to her mother if Koala Lou came in first or last. She would always love her. Her mother knew that Koala Lou tried her best. The author is telling us that our mother will love us no matter what. And she is also telling us that it's important to

In book nooks, students can apply skills and strategies learned in the mini-lesson.

just do your best. That is the author's message or theme of the book. I'm sure you have read many books that have had messages in them. As you read today, I want you to think if there is a message in your book. During share time, we can have you share what you have found."

Developing Mini-Lessons on Literary Techniques

Mini-lessons on literary techniques are also closely tied to the Writing Workshop mini-lessons. In developing the list of topics for your own mini-lessons and in deciding on which books will work best, your goal is always the same: to get students to read like writers. That means teaching them to recognize what authors do to create text; to understand the work that goes into structuring the story; and to appreciate the author's choice of words that create sensory images.

Topics for Mini-Lessons on Literary Techniques

The list below includes suggestions for possible mini-lessons on author's craft and techniques. As you consider the list, notice the close connections between these mini-lessons and those you might use for writing instruction. Use this list in conjunction with the recommended books list (page 96) as you plan your Reading Workshop mini-lessons.

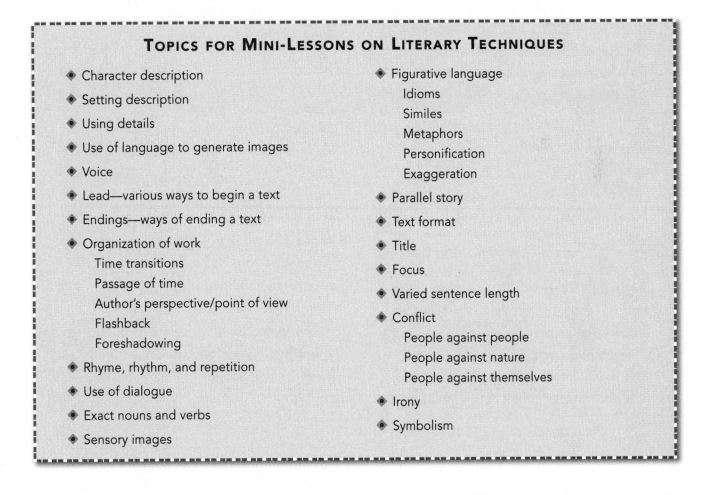

TOPICS FOR MINI-LESSONS ON LITERARY TECHNIQUES

- Character description
- Setting description
- Using details
- Use of language to generate images
- Voice
- Lead—various ways to begin a text
- Endings—ways of ending a text
- Organization of work
    Time transitions
    Passage of time
    Author's perspective/point of view
    Flashback
    Foreshadowing
- Rhyme, rhythm, and repetition
- Use of dialogue
- Exact nouns and verbs
- Sensory images

- Figurative language
    Idioms
    Similes
    Metaphors
    Personification
    Exaggeration
- Parallel story
- Text format
- Title
- Focus
- Varied sentence length
- Conflict
    People against people
    People against nature
    People against themselves
- Irony
- Symbolism

Recommended Books for Mini-Lessons on Literary Techniques

The following list is a good start for books to use to teach author's craft and literary techniques. Picture books are great to use for these mini-lessons. You will soon develop your favorites and will find yourself using them over and over again. The titles in boldface are the more challenging books and/or the chapter books.

RECOMMENDED BOOKS FOR LITERARY TECHNIQUES MINI-LESSONS

Point of View

Carl Makes a Scrapbook by Alexandra Day

The Crocodile and the Dentist by Gomi

Earthlets as Explained by Professor Xargle by Jeanne Willis

First Day Jitters by Julie Danneberg

Grandma According to Me by Karen Magnuson Beil

Hey, Little Ant by Philip M. Hoose

I Am the Dog; I Am the Cat by Donald Hall

Looking for Crabs by Bruce Whatley

Lost by Paul Brett Johnson and Celeste Lewis

My Big Dog by Janet Stevens

Pain and the Great One by Judy Blume

Rover by Michael Rosen

Snow Lambs by Debi Gliori

Figurative Language

Idioms

Amelia Bedelia books by Peggy Parrish

Bunny Money by Rosemary Wells

Similes

Dakota Dugout by Ann Turner

Letting Swift River Go by Jane Yolen

More Than Anything Else by Marie Bradby

Quick as a Cricket by Audrey Wood

Owl Moon by Jane Yolen

Storm in the Night by Mary Stolz

Up North at the Cabin by Marsha Wilson Chall

Metaphors

Dakota Dugout by Ann Turner

Hailstones and Halibut Bones by Mary O'Neill

Knots on a Counting Rope by Bill Martin, Jr.

Nettie's Trip South by Ann Warren Turner

Owl Moon by Jane Yolen

Up North at the Cabin by Marsha Wilson Chall

Personification

I Am the Ocean by Suzanna Marshak

Mrs. Frisby and the Rats of NIMH by Robert C. O'Brien

The Snow Speaks by Nancy White Carlstrom

Velveteen Rabbit by Margery Williams

Where Does the Night Hide? by Nancy White Carlstrom

Books by Marc Brown, Kevin Henkes

Exaggeration

Archibald Frisby by Michael Chesworth

Dirt Boy by Erik Jon Slangerup

Earrings! by Judith Viorst

My Little Sister Ate One Hare by Bill Grossman

There Was an Old Lady Who Swallowed a Fly by Simms Taback

Books by Robert Munsch

Dialogue

Bonaparte by Marsha Wilson Chall

Earrings! by Judith Viorst

Flea Story by Leo Lionni

Make Way for Ducklings by Robert McCloskey

Mouse Told His Mother by Bethany Roberts

Big books by Rigby with color-coded dialogue

Flashback

A Chair for My Mother by Vera Williams

How My Parents Learned to Eat by Allen Say

Miss Rumphius by Barbara Cooney

Sarah Plain and Tall by Patricia MacLachlan

Wringer by Jerry Spinelli

Yolanda's Genius by Carol Fenner

Foreshadowing

The Patchwork Quilt by Valerie Flournoy

Where the Red Fern Grows by Wilson Rawls

Rhyme and Rhythm

Brown Bear, Brown Bear by Bill Martin, Jr.

Chicka, Chicka, Boom, Boom by Bill Martin, Jr.

Chicken Soup with Rice by Maurice Sendak

The Day the Goose Got Loose by Reeve Lindbergh

Each Peach Pear Plum by Janet and Allen Ahlberg

I Can't Said the Ant by Polly Cameron

In the Tall, Tall, Grass by Denise Fleming

In the Small, Small Pond by Denise Fleming

Jesse Bear, What Will You Wear? By Nancy White Carlstrom

Mary Wore Her Red Dress by Merle Peek

Possum Come A-Knockin' by Nancy Van Laan

Tikki Tikki Tembo by Arlene Mosel

The Wheels on the Bus by Maryann Kovalski

Where Do Balloons Go? by Jamie Lee Curtis

Repetition

Aaron's Hair by Robert Munsch

Caps for Sale by Esphyr Slobodkina

A Dark, Dark Tale by Ruth Brown

The Little Red Hen by Paul Galdone

The Runaway Bunny by Margaret Wise Brown

Tikki Tikki Tembo by Arlene Mosel

Sample Literary Techniques Mini-Lesson

Take a look at the following brief lesson on similes. We think this lesson is a good example because it demonstrates how a previously read book can be used for a different purpose. In this instance, Barbara wants these fourth graders to focus on the author's use of similes to create images.

IDENTIFYING SIMILES IN A TEXT

Teacher: We have been learning how authors use different writing techniques to improve the quality of their work. They might be very descriptive or they might write like E.B. White in *Charlotte's Web* and use very exact words to get the point across. Another technique that authors use is the simile. Do you remember when I read the book *Quick as a Cricket* to you?

Student: I like the one where he was as sad as a basset hound.

T: That book gave us some good examples. We talked about the comparisons the author made, you noticed the similes in the book, and then you tried writing some of your own.

TEACHER to TEACHER

Give serious consideration to the level of your students when you choose books for the mini-lessons. While picture books lend themselves to mini-lessons on literary techniques for all grades, be sure to use poetry and chapter books, as well—particularly with students in the upper grades. For example, when teaching a mini-lesson on exact nouns and verbs, read Chapter 3, "Escape," in *Charlotte's Web*. E. B. White was so much the master of choosing just the right words that you can just about smell the barn in this chapter. Or teach a lesson on flashback using *Sarah Plain and Tall* (MacLachlan) or *Wringer* (Spinelli). And, as with all good instruction, sometimes the unexpected happens: During a read aloud of *A Chair for My Mother*, a first-grade student pointed out that the author was telling about a story that happened earlier. This obviously wasn't designed to be a lesson on flashback for first graders, but it turned out to be appropriate to talk about why the author used that technique.

S: Mine was "Her mother said her feet were as quiet as marshmallows."

T: That was a good one. Today I am going to read *Owl Moon* to you, and we will see where the author uses similes to make comparisons and help create images. We have read this book before and talked about the relationship between the father and the child. We also talked about the descriptive language that is used in the book. Now as we read the book, we will pay attention to the similes. When you notice a simile, give a thumbs-up signal.

(As the teacher reads the book, the students give a thumbs-up as they hear a simile. They point out the simile, make the comparisons, and discuss how its use improves the writing.)

T: Today in your reading, see if you notice any similes. If you find one that you would like to share, jot down the page number in your journal and bring the book to share time today.

Lessons like this one carry over to the students' writing. As students notice the author's craft, we also encourage them to apply the techniques to their own writing. We have taught them to "read like writers" and now we guide them as they "write like readers."

CHAPTER 7

READING AS REAL READERS:
Independent Reading, Conferring, Responding, and Sharing

> "What I like most about our Reading Workshop is reading!"
> —Sarah, grade 1

Sarah's quotation says it all—the best part of the Reading Workshop is reading. Students need to practice all that we have taught them. And to do this, they need time to read. They also need time to have conversations about their reading. During the Reading Workshop, students frequently huddle together talking about a book. Or a student may scurry over to a friend to tell him that he's "gotta read this book." This independent reading time is your time to confer with students one on one about their reading. As they open the door and let you into their private reading worlds, listen and respond to their literary needs. It is your opportunity to give students further opportunities to respond in writing and to share their reading experiences with others.

Independent Reading: Behaviors and Practices

After the mini-lesson, as independent reading time begins, students get their books and go off to their own book nooks. During this time they read independently—books of their choice, for their own enjoyment, and which they are capable of reading.

There are a number of key elements that define Reading Workshop independent reading time; these elements enable students to develop as strong independent readers. We discuss each briefly in this section.

Sharing Your Own Passion for Reading

While students are reading at this time, teachers are observing and instructing. Although this means you are not reading along with your students, a critical message to convey to students throughout <u>all</u> of the Reading Workshop—including this period—is your own love of reading. Here are just a few of the opportunities to demonstrate this:

📖 Share the personal reading you do at home. You can do this by bringing in your baskets of books to show students the types of reading you do—or by regularly bringing in books, newspaper articles, and poems that you just *have* to share.

📖 Share your purposes for reading. Let your students know that you have books to read for pleasure, and you also have material that you read for information.

📖 Convey your enthusiasm for the books that you have shared during mini-lessons.

📖 Promote books to read through book talks.

📖 Share reading logs and journals that you personally keep.

📖 Let students know of your enjoyment in visiting bookstores and in discovering books for them and for yourself.

> ### COMPARING DEAR AND READING WORKSHOP INDEPENDENT READING TIME
>
> Although this is independent reading time, it is not DEAR (Drop Everything And Read) time. During DEAR—which can occur at any time during the day—students read books of their choice silently for 15-20 minutes, and typically the teacher often reads along with them. Because the teacher is herself reading, no formal reading instruction takes place. And that is the major difference between DEAR and Reading Workshop independent reading time, when reading instruction not only takes place, but is a major emphasis. In the Reading Workshop, once students have selected "just right" books to read, the teacher is actively engaged in individual and small-group instruction. She might take a running record, assess a student's level of comprehension, listen to a retelling of text, or take part in a story chat as the other children read quietly all around the room.

Orderly Environment

During the 30 to 50 minute period of independent reading, the classroom is quiet and inviting. The students respect each other's reading. The only voices that are heard are reading voices—a student and a teacher in a conference, a teacher conducting a guided reading group, or students reading and discussing a book together. In an area away from most of the students, a small group of children may be meeting for a story chat. Students have their materials with them. If they must return a book to the classroom library and get another, they do so in a way that does not disrupt the others.

Book Choice

Teaching children how to choose a just right book is important. During independent reading time, students should read books with which they are comfortable. You can help them make decisions when they may need to challenge themselves a little more. In addition, provide guidance to make sure they are reading a variety of genres. You'll sometimes need to steer some students to nonfiction material while finding other genres for the student who only seems to read science fiction.

Reading With Others

Reading is a social experience. You can provide for social reading by encouraging communication between readers during independent reading time. Students may participate in guided reading or flexible skill groups, partner reading, or in a small literature response group or "story chat." In short, you need to be sure that your students have authentic reading experiences and opportunities to talk about their books and their thinking.

Partner reading (see the box below) is an excellent example of how social an experience reading can be. In the first part of the box, we describe what partner reading is; after that we recommend modeling a mini-lesson on partner reading (with another adult) so your students will know your expectations.

PARTNER READING

What Is It?

Partner reading is very popular in primary classrooms. Often students have similar interests and want to read a book together. Sometimes each student has his or her own copy, but typically they share a book. These students are usually at the same reading level and enjoy the same types of books. They decide how to share the reading, maybe alternating pages. By listening in on how the students assist one another, you can assess the strategies they feel comfortable using. For example, one partner my offer the other help, saying, "That word starts like your name, Frank" or "Do you see the 'ing' chunk?"

At the upper grades, students still participate in partner reading, but it may look different, especially if the readers are proficient. Students at these levels may read silently next to each other and stop occasionally to discuss what has happened.

Modeling Reading with a Partner

1. *Find a place to read:* Decide quietly together where the best place would be to read together. Go there quickly.

2. *Demonstrate quiet voices:* Talk so only you and your partner can hear each other. Demonstrate both appropriate and inappropriate voices.

3. *Demonstrate how to share one copy of a book:* Decide how the book will be held and who will turn the pages. (Model compromise of taking turns to turn pages.)

4. *Model beginning predictions, how to talk about what we think the book might be about:* Point out how you are acting like good listeners (eye contact, nods, quiet hands and feet). Also model an example of poor listeners.

5. *Model plan making:* "Let's read this book first today and this one next. Let's stop to retell at the end of every other page. How about you read the left side and I'll read the right side."

6. *Model wait time:* "If my partner gets stuck on a word, I should not blurt out the answer. I should ask questions about how we might solve the problem together." Model a good example and a poor example.

7. *Model the retelling:* "Let's stop here since we planned on it. I just finished reading, so you retell what has happened while I was reading aloud. After you finish reading, we'll stop and it will be my turn to retell."

Story Chats

As you already know, children enjoy reading together. However, you want them to do more than just read together. You want them to discuss the book, to share questions and confusions they have, and to make connections between this book and other books they are reading or to their own lives. In order to make this time productive, guide the students to carefully choose a book that they can read together. Model for them what you would do in a story chat so that they can see what readers do when they discuss books.

It helps to provide a set of questions and a reading/thinking guide for students to get started with story chats. We've had success with the forms below (blank templates of these for your use are on pages 156 and 157). It's instructive to look at Kristina's filled-in forms below—an example of the kind of thoughtful response to books we're always delighted to see.

TEACHER to TEACHER

In order to encourage dialogue about books, you can steer several students to the same title. Or some students can hold discussions on books that have a common author, theme, or genre. The students can decide if they will read together or if they will meet for discussion at a particular point. The level of independence of this task depends on the level of maturity of the students—no matter what the grade level.

Name Kristina   Date 6-12-02

Story Chats

Book Title Tuck Everlasting
Author Natalie Babbitt

Before meeting with your group:
- Note things you want to discuss (you can use sticky notes).
- Write down any confusing parts (or use sticky notes).
- Write questions you want to ask the group.

Are you prepared for your Story Chat?
- ☑ I have read the book (or the assigned part).
- ☑ I have noted things to discuss.
- ☑ I have noted confusing parts.
- ☑ I have questions to ask the group.

One thing we need to discuss in our Story Chat is:
Mae killed the man in the yellow suit.

These were things I was confused about:
1. The toad
2. The man in the yellow suit
3. When Tuck put Winnie in the boat

Here are questions I will ask:
1. What are gallows?
2. Why is the constable important?
3. Why did the man in the yellow suit not have a name?
4. Why did the man in the yellow suit wear a yellow suit?
5. Did Winnie's family know about the spring?

Name Kristina   Date 6-12-02

After the Story Chat

Three things that I learned or were helpful from the Story Chat:
1. I learned what Gallows are
2. How Tuck explained the life cycle to the water
3. Michelle and Amanda were also confused.

These are things we should do differently for our next meeting:
letting someone else each time start off talking about the book

Our next assignment is: ch. 21 - to end

Guided Reading

During independent reading time, teachers often meet students in small, guided reading groups (see description below). This is typically most helpful in the primary grades and for students reading below grade level. However, it obviously cuts into time for conferring individually with students. You may want to see if there is support available—for example, a reading specialist, a special education teacher, a resource/support teacher, a teacher assistant, or a trained volunteer. These extra hands can assist you by conferring with the students.

Marybeth leads a first-grade group in guided reading.

WHAT IS GUIDED READING?

"Guided reading is a teaching approach designed to help individual students learn how to process a variety of increasingly challenging texts with understanding and fluency. Guided reading occurs in a small-group context because the small group allows for interactions among readers that benefit them all. The teacher selects and introduces texts to readers, sometimes supports them while reading the text, engages the readers in a discussion, and makes teaching points after the reading. Sometimes, after reading a text, the teacher extends the meaning of the text through writing, text analysis, or another learning experience. The lesson also may include work with words based on the specific needs of the group."
(Fountas and Pinnell, *Guiding Readers and Writers*, Grades 3-6, 2001)

TEACHER to TEACHER

Having parent volunteers help out in your classroom is a wonderful thing. However, often teachers end up spending precious time preparing materials and activities for the volunteer. In our Reading Workshop we have virtually eliminated the questions, "What will the volunteers do in my classroom?" and "How will I train them?" We have created a form (see page 104) that helps teachers and volunteers communicate with one another without any wasted minutes. The classroom teacher takes only a few minutes to jot down students who may need extra attention during independent reading time, and what skills or strategies should be focused on. When the volunteer arrives, he simply picks up a clipboard with the form on it and follows the directives of the teacher. Volunteers are free to jot down any notes or thoughts they had as they read with the students.

Reading Workshop Helpers

Thanks for being here! When you read with the students today, please focus your attention on the following students. But please don't feel as if these are the only students to read with. We all love to read with a partner!

Student:	Volunteer Comments:
Strategies:	
Student:	Volunteer Comments:
Strategies:	
Student:	Volunteer Comments:
Strategies:	
Student:	Volunteer Comments:
Strategies:	
Student:	Volunteer Comments:
Strategies:	

Revisiting the Reading Workshop: Management, Mini-Lessons, and Strategies • Scholastic Professional Books

Flexible Grouping

When teaching specific skills, it makes sense to assemble only those students who are in need of extra practice with the particular skill. Spending time re-teaching students skills that they already have a handle on does them a disservice. For this reason, it's a good idea to form flexible groups—small groups that meet as needed during quiet reading time. These are not necessarily ability level groups. It's quite possible, probable even, to form a group that includes a very high reader and a very low reader. The idea is to focus on one skill only and to invite everyone in the room who still needs extra practice with that skill. You might also form a flexible group aimed at enriching students who have all mastered a certain skill or strategy. (See the box below for a listing of reasons to consider forming a flexible group.)

As you conference, continually think about the needs of each individual reader. If, while you are reading with a student, you notice a particular strength or weakness that could be addressed in a small group, take note of the skill or strategy and list the student's name on a Small Group Planning Page. Throughout the next couple of days, as you conference, note whether there are other readers who would benefit from the small group, or groups, you are planning. If so, list that child's name in the appropriate place. When you have a couple of names, plan the group and call students together during the next quiet reading time.

PLANNING FOR SMALL GROUPS (AM)

Chapter book hand holding	Daily Word Work	Fluency
Brian	Jonathan	Brianna
Kristina	Tony	Tori Andrew
Kirstie	Andrew	Devin
	Earl	Kristina
		Jessica
Comp. Strats. self-monitoring	Judging/Forming Opinions	Stick with it ness
Tamika	Paige	Joe
Brianna	Kirstie	Tori
Joey	Kristina	Tony
	Jessica	
Assessing self-strategies	Writing Responses	Using Word Wall
•Mandy	Tony	Earl
•Brittani	Brianna	Jonathan
•Meagan	Tori	

REASONS TO HOLD SMALL FLEXIBLE GROUPS

Hold a small flexible group when you note that extra work is needed in any of these areas:

◆ Fluency

◆ Word work

◆ Decoding multisyllabic words

◆ Decoding new words using chunks already familiar

◆ Using context clues to figure out new words

◆ Story sequencing

◆ Retelling the story using story elements

◆ Using context clues

◆ Forming opinions about the reading

◆ Stronger journal responses

◆ When to abandon a book

◆ Reading chapter books in their entirety

◆ Using all reading time wisely

◆ Selecting a new book based on personal interest

◆ Any topic that has already been presented to the whole class as a mini-lesson

When holding these small flexible groups, remember the following pointers:

📖 Students should not lose all of their reading time because they are participating in a small skill group. Often, it is these students who need the most practice with actual text. Make the group short and to the point. Be sure to zero in on one skill and one skill only.

📖 When possible, use poetry and excerpts of text to illuminate your point. These lend themselves easily to a shortened lesson.

📖 At the conclusion of the group, give students something to hang onto as a reminder of the theme of the group: a sticky note with the topic sentence written on it, a bookmark with key strategies, an idea recorded in their reading journal, etc.

📖 Consider giving students a skill to practice or a job to do and meet with that same group again that week to check on their progress and assess their ability to apply the skill or strategy in their own reading.

📖 Remember that these groups are flexible. Try not to pull the same students over and over again in the same group. If students are truly that needy, then a daily guided reading group would better serve their needs.

Conferring With Students: "How's It Going?"

By conferencing with a student, you can understand the student's reading process and provide individualized instruction. Before this effective conferencing can take place, students must know how to read independently—and that means they need to read quietly. They must respect you and the student with whom you are conferring so that you are not disturbed. Make sure you have spent enough time preparing your students for independent reading as well as preparing them for conferences. Your students must know what you expect out of their behavior when they read and also when they confer with you. You can model for your students and have some students role-play the behaviors you expect during quiet, independent reading.

What a Conference Looks and Feels Like

During a conference, pull up a chair and sit close to the reader so that you are on the same level. This may be at the student's desk or in his or her book nook. Although some teachers prefer to have students come to them at a table, we prefer physically moving around the room, conferring with students in what may appear—to them—to be a "random" pattern. This enables us to confer with individuals based on their needs and not just because "it's Jennifer's turn since we just met with Jason."

> **TEACHER to TEACHER**
>
> Sometimes students need lots of reminders to give you your space while you are conferencing or leading a small group. In our lower grade Reading Workshops, we've resolved this problem with the use of a hat. After reading the book *Koala Lou* to students, we lead them to understand that even though we love them dearly, we cannot possibly be with each student every single time we are needed. Inspired by the read aloud story, we attach a tag to an interesting hat that says, "I do love you...not now." At the start of independent reading time, we put on our hat. Students can see from across the room that since the teacher has her hat on, now's not the best time to disturb her!

When you pull up for a conference, encourage the reader to carry on with what he is doing. This provides some time for additional assessment. Through observation (or from your notes from a previous conference), determine what the student is doing and what your focus is for that conference. Ask yourself questions such as:

📖 Is the student appropriately engaged with the text or group reading?

📖 Is his/her text level appropriate?

📖 Is the student applying the strategies you last taught him or her?

📖 Is he/she easily distracted by others or by other activities in the room?

📖 Is the student relying on reading with someone else?

📖 Is he/she using a finger or a bookmark to help keep his/her place during reading?

Careful observation provides the on-the-spot lesson for that particular student. It can also provide information about whether or not you should include him or her in a small group lesson. Thinking about all of your reading conferences of the day can even help you plan the next day's mini-lesson for the class. (See Chapter 8 for detailed information about observation and assessment.)

As you find a place to enter a child's reading, start off simply by saying something like, "How's it going?" By whispering or talking in low voices, you can avoid disturbing others around you. Although conferences may be very brief, even just two or three minutes, they also can be up to eight minutes in length. It's a good idea to go to a student conference armed with materials: a notebook with record-keeping forms, clipboards with note cards for anecdotal records, a dry erase board, sticky notes, bookmarks, and even magnetic letters.

When you begin a conference, aim for a positive opening by recognizing something the child is doing well. "Tony, I noticed you've started another book" or "Tamika, I can tell you like books by Marc Brown." It's best to be honest in providing students with specific feedback—this means telling them if a selected book is too hard and helping them make better choices.

A parent volunteer assists a fifth grader during independent reading.

You might point out what the child did during reading, such as if he or she self-corrected a word when it didn't make sense. What you teach a child during the conference is based on your close observations of the reading work the child is doing. Listen as the child reads a passage and observe how he or she handles reading errors. And listen to the child's retelling of a story or interpretation of the book.

During a conference, you might ask the child to read a portion of the text aloud, tell about the events in the story, share a journal response, or make a connection to the day's mini-lesson. Converse with the student as one reader to another and ask genuine questions. Based on your on-the-spot assessment or from previous assessments, you'll determine one or two teaching points and provide the student with individualized direct instruction. (The boxes below give you some further pointers about holding successful conferences.) •

IMPORTANT POINTS ABOUT CONFERENCES: BEHAVIORS AND ROLES

◆ Respect student's reading. There are times when you'll attempt to enter into a conference only to have a student say, "Not right now, I'm at a really good part in my book." We've all had the experience of reading a book and not wanting to be disturbed, and teachers must respect the students who simply must read that "really good part." At your next conference, you can learn about that good part.

◆ Conferences with students will vary. Don't worry about the length of a conference and don't have a timer nearby to limit your conferences or to keep them to one standard length. Although you want to touch base with as many students as possible, sometimes giving extra time to the student who needs a longer conference is called for.

◆ For those very capable readers, meet their needs and challenge them. Give them opportunities to choose higher quality literature, to try a different genre, to have higher-level discussions, and to stretch their reading level.

◆ In a conference, both the teacher and the student have important roles to play. The teacher does not do all of the talking, and the student is not just a passive recipient of information. Confer with your students as one reader to another.

TEACHER'S ROLE IN CONFERENCE

◆ Learns about student's reading interests
◆ Determines appropriateness of text
◆ Observes strategies used while reading
◆ Listens to oral reading
◆ Takes running record
◆ Asks questions of reading
◆ Determines level of engagement
◆ Discusses book with student
◆ Listens to what student is saying about reading
◆ Determines a "teaching point"
◆ Shares her assessment
◆ Keeps a record of the conference
◆ Provides a focus for the child's reading and the next conference

STUDENT'S ROLE IN CONFERENCE

◆ Informs teacher of interests
◆ Is prepared with materials
◆ Applies strategies to reading
◆ Reads orally if asked
◆ Retells, responds, reflects
◆ Demonstrates understanding, provides evidence for support
◆ Discusses book with teacher
◆ Explains any confusions
◆ Decides what to share from reading
◆ Participates in the instruction
◆ Listens to the assessment
◆ Asks how to improve
◆ Determines goals with teacher

Three-Part Model

In conferencing with students, keep in mind the three-part model of Lucy Calkins (2001).

1. *Research* what the child can do as a reader.

2. *Decide* what needs to be taught.

3. *Teach* in a way that will influence what the child will do independently.

This model will help you remember that your goal is to teach the reader something that will make a difference in his or her continued reading, not just in a particular piece of text.

Keeping Track

The Individual Conference Form (see page 110) can help you keep track of your student conferences. You'll probably find this form especially beneficial as you begin conferencing with your students. Your use of this form will change throughout the year as you gain more confidence with conferences and as you get to know your students.

Different Times for Conferring

Since you do not meet with every student individually on a daily basis, you wind up observing different students at different stages throughout the reading process. You might meet before a student begins a new book and help, if necessary, in the selection of the book. You can also observe how the student previews the book, sets a purpose for reading, and activates prior knowledge. If you meet with the student midway through a book, you will have an opportunity to assess his or her comprehension of the text and see how the student makes connections. You may even meet as a student completes a book, at which time you can ask him or her to reflect on the book, draw conclusions, and compare the book to others. Checking in with your readers at all of these importance stages helps you to form a more complete picture of how each reader in your room operates.

Different Types of Conferences

In the beginning of the year, your conferences will help you get to know your students. You'll hear about their personal interests and experiences and learn about their attitudes toward reading. Soon after the year starts, conferences will help you look more closely at students as readers, enabling you to determine the level of support each student needs.

Although one of the easiest ways to start a conference with a student is by asking, "How's it going?" you may want to be more specific as you meet with particular students. On page 111 we describe different types of conferences, along with suggested opening statements and questions.

Individual Conference Form

Book Title _____   **Page** _____

Initial Observations: _____

_____

"Can you tell me a little about what's going on in your book right now?"

Notes on the retelling: _____

_____

Affect:	☐ excited	☐ bored	☐ confused
Information supplied:	☐ big picture of story		☐ zeroes in on minor details
	☐ relies on pictures/captions for retelling		
Overall retelling:	☐ strong	☐ average	☐ poor

"May I read quietly with you for a while?" or "Could you read to me a little from where you left off?"

Notes on the reading: _____

_____

Comprehension check: ☐ strong   ☐ average   ☐ poor

Evidence of strategy use: _____

_____

Other notes: _____

_____

One teaching point to share: _____

_____

Student's goal/job before the next conference: _____

_____

Revisiting the Reading Workshop: Management, Mini-Lessons, and Strategies • Scholastic Professional Books

Getting to Know You

These conferences help you learn about your students' reading interests and attitudes. Suggested openers and questions include:

- Do you like books by this author?

- I see you're reading a biography. What others types of books do you like?

- Is this a "just-right" book for you? How can you tell?

- Tell me what you like best about reading.

- Which book on your reading list is your favorite? Why?

- I want to just listen to you read a little bit.

- Tell me what has happened so far.

- Is this character at all like you? Why or why not?

Content/Comprehension

In these conferences you discuss the book and focus on the student's understanding. Suggested openers and questions include:

- What are some important points to remember from this chapter/book?

- Can you make some connections between this book and yourself? Between this book and other books?

- Tell me what's been going on so far.

- What have you learned about the main character(s)?

- Why is the setting important to this story?

- Are there any parts here that don't make sense?

- What have you learned so far?

- What's the main problem in the story?

- Do you have any questions about the story?

Format

These conferences focus on the various types of reading genres and text formats. At this time you can call attention to the use of pictures, graphs, charts, the table of contents, index, etc. Suggested openers and questions include:

- How is the text format of the book like the one we read today in our mini-lesson?

- Do you prefer this genre? Why?

- How did the pictures/diagrams help you understand the book?

- Have you read other books/poetry by this author? How do they compare?

- Why did you choose this particular book?

- Why do you think the author set up the text in this type of format?

- Why is this chapter called _____?

- How do the headings and subheadings help?

- I noticed you used the table of contents. How did it help you?

Reading Process

These conferences help you learn what the child does as a reader—the strategies used, the connections made, and the books selected. Below are suggested openers and questions for several types of reading process conferences—decoding, fluency, and strategic reading.

Decoding:

- I'd like to listen to you read a little bit. Then we can talk about your reading.

- Does that sound right?

- Does that make sense?

- What part of this word do you know?

- What part of this word confuses you?

- Is there a chunk in that word that you know?

- That's a long word. Let's break it into parts.

- Look at the whole word, not just the beginning of the word.

Fluency:

- Make the reading sound like talking.

- Listen to me read these sentences. Then we'll read it together.

- You aren't pausing at the end of the sentences. Let's try this together.

- Let's try reading in phrases—not word by word, but groups of words together.

- Try reading without pointing to the words. That's slowing you down.

- Now that you practiced reading that page, try it again a little faster.

Strategic Reading:

- Does this book remind you of any other books you know?

- This book doesn't have any pictures. What are you seeing in your head?

- Can you find a part to read to me that helped you visualize what is going on?

- Is anything confusing to you as you read this?

- How can I help your reading today?

- What do you think will happen next? Why do you think so?

- What connections are you making to your own life?

- Are you making any connections to other books you've read or books I've read to you?

Assessment

While you are constantly assessing the reader in all conferences, you may design conferences aimed specifically at providing you with information on fluency, comprehension, and strategic reading. (See Chapter 8 for more about assessment.) Suggested openers and questions for this type of conference are:

- Can you summarize in your own words the chapter you just read?

- What are some important points that you need to remember in this chapter?

- What do you think the author's message is?

- Why do you think the author wrote this book?

- I'm going to listen to you read for a bit. I'll be taking some notes and then we'll talk about your reading.

- What in your reading today can you connect with our mini-lesson?

- I'd like you to read up to here, and then I want you to retell what happened in the story.

- What do you think you are best at in reading?

- Share a part in the book you really liked.

- What do you think you could do to be an even better reader?

Teacher Interventions for Students With Reading Difficulties

As you observe and confer with students, you can act as a reading coach to your students. You'll follow their lead, offering guidance and instruction, when and where they need it. The chart on pages 113–114 offers interventions to consider, especially as you work with students with reading difficulties.

TEACHER INTERVENTIONS FOR READING DIFFICULTIES

Student Behavior	Teacher Intervention	Possible Feedback
Reader constantly abandons text.	Assist with book selection, highlighting books at the appropriate readability and interest level.	*What kinds of books do you like to read?* *Is this a "just right" book?* *Is this a "vacation" book?* *Is this a "dream" book?* *Did you use the 5-finger test to choose a book?*
Reader spends more time browsing than reading.	Teacher assists with book choice and closely monitors initial reading of text.	*Let me help you choose a book.* *Let's take a few minutes together while you read this book.* *Read this page and then stop and tell me what happened.*
Student selects book that is too difficult.	Help student find book on the same topic that is easier to read. Adult can read the more difficult book with the student. Assist student in strategy for future book selection, e.g. the five-finger test.	*I can tell you are interested in reading about _____.* *This book may be a little difficult, but I can help you find another book on _____.* *Is this a book you want to read with someone?* *Let me tell you what I do to choose a book* • *5-finger test* • *read first page and then read in middle of the book*
Student sounds like a reader but demonstrates little comprehension of text.	Points to ponder: • interest level • prior knowledge • ask to think /pause/retell • determine where comprehension breaks down (sentence, paragraph, page)	*What do you know about this subject?* *Is this a topic that interests you?* *Stop here and think about what you just read.* *Are there any words that confused you?*
Student constantly chooses books that are too easy.	Teacher acknowledges student interest (e.g. mystery, nonfiction) but guides to more appropriate level while continuing to provide support.	*This looks like another "vacation" book.* *It looks like you are interested in _____.* *Let's find another book on _____ when you finish this one. See me if you need help finding a book that's a "just right" book.*
Reader doesn't plan before reading.	Teacher models effective strategies such as: previewing, listing, mapping, asking questions, recalling prior knowledge.	*Before I start reading, I think about what I already know about the topic.* *I ask myself questions that I want answered in the book.* *If there's a book jacket, I read it to try to figure out what the book might be about.*
Reader doesn't set a purpose before reading.	Teacher reminds student of purposes for reading (to be informed, entertained, persuaded). Models strategies such as: identifying task, asking questions, making predictions.	*Why do you think the author wrote this book?* *Do you think this book will inform, entertain, or persuade you?* *Before I start reading, I think of why I'm reading this book—interest, assignment.*

Student Behavior	Teacher Intervention	Possible Feedback
Reader shows excellent listening comprehension but has difficulty with comprehension when reading independently.	Teacher checks appropriateness of readability. Teacher models comprehension strategies.	*You really seemed interested when I was reading.* *You really understood what I was reading. I'm going to show you what I do when I am trying to understand what I read (choose strategy to model).*
Reader has inadequate background knowledge to be successful with text.	Teacher needs to provide background information (e.g. artifacts, maps, videos, experiences).	*What do you know about _____?* *Let's see if this book has some pictures that will help us try to understand what _____ looks like.* *I think I have something at home that I can bring in to help you understand about _____.*
Reader doesn't ask questions.	Teacher models questioning strategy showing how to question before, during, and after reading.	*When I read I am constantly asking questions. I ask questions <u>before</u> I start reading but I ask more questions <u>during</u> reading. <u>After</u> reading, I ask how I felt about the characters, events, the ending. I also ask questions if I am confused.*
Reader doesn't make predictions.	Teacher shares how to make predictions based on pictures, prior knowledge, and experiences. Also shows how to revise predictions.	*Good readers make predictions because of what they already know about a topic and the experiences they've had. Good readers also revise and adjust their predictions.*
Reader reads literally, doesn't make inferences.	Teacher models strategy for making inferences based on prior knowledge and from information in text.	*Readers sometimes have to act like a detective. Authors don't tell you everything. You have to read between the lines and try to figure things out.*
Reader doesn't visualize.	Teacher models a think aloud explaining what she visualizes based on descriptions from text.	*A good writer helps me get pictures in my head while I'm reading. I think about what the author is describing in the text.*
Student doesn't focus on major content.	Teacher assists student in monitoring comprehension by rereading when confused, adjusting rate of reading, taking notes, and using sticky notes and bookmarks.	*When I read nonfiction books, I read differently than when I read fiction. I slow down my rate of reading. Sometimes I take notes when I'm trying to remember information. I even use sticky notes or bookmarks.*
Reader doesn't reflect on passage.	Teacher models a think aloud demonstrating her reflections on text.	*As I read, I stop and reflect on what I've read. I might do that after a paragraph, a page, or even a chapter.*
Reader has difficulty remembering and summarizing.	Teacher models responding in a journal. Also provides opportunities for relating the new material to known material.	*To help me remember what I've read, I respond in a journal. I write questions I have, confusions I have, things that affect me personally, things I disagree with, things I really enjoy and want to remember.*

Two Extended Sample Reading Conferences

As you conference, you respond to the student even as you continually make mental notes of concerns and ideas for instruction. Take a look at the student conference below on the book *The Chocolate Touch*. The teacher's mental notes and ongoing assessment decisions are included for you to consider.

MAKING MENTAL NOTES DURING A READING CONFERENCE: HELPING STUDENTS TO STOP, QUESTION, AND THINK DURING READING

Teacher: How's it going today?

Student: Okay. I think. I'm on the second chapter of the book already.

(A warning bell goes off for the teacher, because the student shared only where he was in the book, not what was going on in the story.)

T: Can you help me understand what's been going on in your book so that I can keep reading it with you?

S: Well, John found some money in the road and he's buying some chocolate from Africa.

(The student has zeroed in on a minor detail. The teacher senses that the main ideas are being overlooked. She decides to revisit the questioning strategy with him.)

T: What are you wondering about at this point in the story?

S: Um...what kind of chocolate will he buy?

T: Hmmm. You know one of the strategies that good readers use that helps them understand all that the author is trying to say is questioning. Do you remember any mini-lessons that we talked about questioning?

S: Let's see. I remember that we kept asking questions about that book that had those riots in it.

T: Yes, we asked questions while we were reading *Smoky Night* and that helped us to better understand the story. Have you been asking questions in your head as you read about John Midas in your book today?

S: Not really.

T: Well, how about we ask some questions together to help you get started?

S: Okay.

T: Let's back up to where John found the money.

S: *(Student reads text.)* "On the one side there was a picture of a fat boy; on the other side were the letters J.M.—which was funny, John thought, because those letters happened to be his initials."

T: Okay. Slow your reading down. Don't just plow through. Let's think. Are you wondering anything right now?

S: Well, I've never seen any money like that before. It must not be real.

T: Right. You're asking, "Is it real or not?"

S: And, I wonder where it came from, since it has John's initials on it.

T: Yes! I'm also wondering, or asking myself in my head, whether John was meant to find it, or if it's just a big coincidence. Let's keep reading. Sometimes, your questions will be answered right in the book.

S: "…I'm going a new way."

T: Stop and think. What are you wondering?

S: Well, why would John go a new way this time?

T: That's what good readers do. They keep thinking in their head as they read. Go on.

S: *(Student continues to read.)*

T: *(Teacher sits and listens, perhaps quietly prompting student to stop and think until the student is able to remember to ask questions on his own.)*

T: This is such a good book. I'm so glad you'll be enjoying it more because you'll be stopping and asking questions. Tell me, in your own words, what we talked about today in this conference.

S: That I need to go slow and remember to think about the words in my head and the author's words both at the same time.

T: Yes, that's exactly what good readers do. I'm going to give you this sticky note to remind you that good readers slow down their reading and ask questions about the book. (On a sticky note, teacher writes, "Good readers slow down to ask questions about the story.") Use this as a bookmark for a while until you remember to do that all on your own. When we meet for our next conference, I'm going to ask you to tell me how you have been better at using this strategy. Okay? Enjoy the book.

The following conference took place while a student was reading the book *Stone Fox*. It includes the conference dialogue between the teacher and a student, in addition to the teacher's mental notes.

MAKING MENTAL NOTES DURING A READING CONFERENCE: HELPING STUDENTS TO USE CLUES AND SELF-MONITORING TO MAKE MEANING

Teacher: How's it going?

Student: Pretty good. I just started another book. Sam recommended it.

(The teacher hopes it's not too hard for the student, because it's such a good story.)

T: Wow! *Stone Fox.* That's a great book. Is it a just right book for you?

S: I think so. I haven't had much trouble so far—just with the long words.

(Teacher notices the mention of the long words, and realizes that she's going to have to look at this text together with the student.)

T: Just the long words. What do you do then?

S: Sometimes I try to chunk them up.

T: Does that help?

S: Yeah.

(Teacher knows she needs to see if he's understanding the story.)

T: Tell me what's going on so far.

S: Willy's worried about his grandfather. He doesn't know if he's sick or just playing a trick on him like he sometimes does.

(Teacher thinks, "Wow, that's a pretty good summary for the first couple of pages.")

T: What do you think is going on?

S: I don't know. I need to read and find out.

T: Where did you leave off?

S: Right here.

T: Let me listen in as you read a bit.

S: (page 5) "Searchlight was a big black dog.... ...which was over ten years ago." That's not too old, is it?

T: It doesn't seem too old.

(Teacher thinks the student sounds pretty good and notices that he's questioning as he's reading.)

T: Keep reading.

S: "A mile down the road... Doc Smith had snow white hair and wore a long black dress." Wait a minute. Why does the doctor have a dress on?

T: Keep reading to find out.

S: "Her skin was tan and her face was covered with wrinkles." The doctor's a woman?

T: Yes, women are doctors, too.

S: But that's not what I was picturing.

T: You were picturing something?

S: Yeah, in my head. I saw a man doctor.

T: Sometimes the pictures we create are different than the text. Keep reading.

S: "...his harmonica? she asked." What's a harmonica? A game?

T: Back up to here and read it again. See if you get a clue.

S: Something with music? An instrument?

T: Yes, it is a musical instrument. It's rectangular and it has holes along one long end and you blow into it with your mouth and make music.

S: Oh, I know what that is. I saw a country and western band use them.

T: Good. Now you can picture it. You used the clues that the author gave you right in the story. That was just like my mini-lesson today. I figured out what words meant by using the clue words in the story.

(Teacher decides that these are good teaching points for him today, makes a note to follow-up with the student on these, and decides to listen just a little bit more.)

S: "...full of tears." *(Student pronounces it to rhyme with cares.)* Why is his beard full of tears? That doesn't make sense.

T: You're thinking like a good reader. You are questioning when something doesn't make sense. Let's look at that word again. I see "ears" in this word.

S: Ears, t - ears, tears. Oh, tears! That makes sense.

T: Read that sentence again now.

S: *(continues, then)* I get a different picture in my head.

(Teacher thinks, "Great! He's visualizing the reading.")

T: I think you're going to like this book. Remember, reading has to make sense. Keep doing what good readers do. Use the clues the author gives for new words and ask questions when the reading doesn't make sense. I'll check in with you tomorrow to see how the book is coming.

The above conferences are particularly effective for a number of reasons. First, the teachers were constantly involved in assessment—determining what the reader was doing and what the student needed. Second, these conferences followed the pattern of Calkins's three-part model recommended earlier: "Research, Decide, Teach." And third, the teachers delivered instruction aimed at the student's overall reading, not just one particular text.

Responding and Sharing

Response is a vital component of the Reading Workshop. The numerous opportunities for thoughtful response that characterize the Workshop culminate in the more structured response time that happens during and after independent reading and conferring. This is a dedicated time for conversations about reading, with the teacher and with peers. It is also a time set aside for personal reflection and written response. And, at the end of the Reading Workshop, the classroom reading community comes together to share and celebrate their reading successes. As Sharon Taberski (2000) states, "After all, the primary purpose of responding to books is to move children into a richer and a broader reading experience. And as children read more widely and more proficiently, they can respond more effectively" (p. 171).

Conversations About Reading

We are so fortunate to be in a profession where we have opportunities for daily conversations about books—time to talk about books with colleagues and with students. Think of the many times during the course of the day when you and your students converse about books. As stated earlier, reading may <u>seem</u> like a quiet, isolated activity, but it should be considered a social time. Talking about what you've read gives you and your students a chance to relive the experience. And you need to show your students how to do this. Students need to listen to the ideas of others, to develop their critical thinking skills, and to explore their literary interpretations with others.

Too often teachers spend time only on having students respond in writing to their reading and to answer questions after they read. But students need to talk about books during the whole reading process—before, during, and after reading. And they need to have conversations about books with their peers, not just with the teacher. In your teaching role, you can guide the students in their dialogue about books. Sometimes these discussions can be very informal; other times they may be more focused. In this way students can learn how to articulate their thoughts, to justify their opinions, and to support their interpretations by providing evidence or background information. Through developing a respect for one another, readers learn to consider the perspectives of others while agreeing or disagreeing.

Responding Through Writing

In addition to encouraging students to converse about their reading, it is important to provide them with sufficient time for written response. The writing process gives students personal, uninterrupted time to interpret and reflect on the text they've just read. Before taking a detailed look at the primary means of written student response—*reading response journals*—let's first examine something more mundane: the materials you'll want to have on hand to allow your students to do their best thinking and writing.

MATERIALS NEEDED

◆ *Reading journals.* Marbled composition books work well for students' writing about their thoughts, feelings, and reactions. They can use these journals to record memorable language, confusing vocabulary, or page numbers of passages they want to share.

◆ *Sticky notes.* These allow students to mark places they want to share. They also can jot a brief note about a particular piece of text. Teach students to be frugal and divide sticky notes into smaller sections or re-use them. See the note below.

Use Sticky Notes to mark:

where you have a question.

a part you would like to come back to and talk about.

a favorite line.

a part you can really see.

a lock: a place where the book is hard to understand.

a key—a place where the book answers one of your questions.

where it connects to another book.

where it connects to something in your life.

where you can really feel the story.

a very important part.

a place that helps you predict.

a part that makes you wonder.

a special part with interesting language.

vocabulary that you don't understand.

a part you don't like or believe.

a part that you think is funny.

◆ *Bookmarks.* These are used like the sticky notes. Students can write page numbers and other ideas on them.

◆ *Highlighters.* Although these are not used as often because texts are usually shared, teach students how to use highlighters with their own texts or with handout copies.

Reading Response Journals

Students should keep reading response journals for recording their thoughts, questions, feelings, and personal connections. Response journals work best when students know what is expected of them. If you take the time to model what a journal entry should look like, it will pay off many times over. And be sure to post the models in your classroom so that students can refer to them as they write.

Our primary students tend to wait until the end of independent reading time and then, with directions from the teacher, write a response to the day's reading. As you can see in the two examples at the bottom of this page, these young readers will respond well to both general directions such as, "Write about your favorite part" or to more focused prompts like, "Write a connection you made to yourself in the story you read."

Modeling what you expect—even the inclusion of the date and title—is key. Take a look at the early second-grade example at the top of page 121. The components listed in parentheses represent those items that the teacher has required of all students and modeled for them, regardless of what book they were reading.

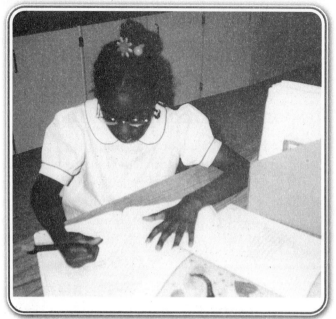

A third grader's journal reflects her use of strategies.

TEACHER to TEACHER
First-grade teachers may want to wait until early winter to begin asking students to write about what is read. However, it is never too soon to model this type of writing or to do interactive and shared writing activities that help students learn to write about their reading.

Nov 15
The Great Snake
Escape
I liked the part when
the goos was holding
the ferg.

Loah

7-12
Feb.7
In Fluffy Goes To Washing-
ton it remembered me of when
I went to Washington.

Alexandra F.

(date)	October 5
(title)	Today I read Lilly's Purple Plastic Purse.
(favorite part)	My favorite part was when her teacher wrote Lilly a note.
(reason)	I liked that part because I know the teacher understood how Lilly felt.

In later second grade or third grade, the teacher may want the students to be able to identify the literary elements of the story. Again, it is important for the teacher to give the students a model, as demonstrated in the following example.

(date)	January 15
(title)	Amazing Grace
(main characters)	Grace, her grandmother
(setting)	Grace's school and house
(main idea)	Students in Grace's class tell her that she can't be Peter Pan in the school play because she is a girl and is black. Her grandmother takes her to see a famous ballerina. Grace learns she can be whatever she wants to be.

In a third- or fourth-grade classroom, the teacher may want the student to write a cohesive paragraph with a clear beginning, some thoughts and questions, and a closing. The following example shows some specific expectations.

(date)	November 10
(title)	A Dog Called Kitty
(page I began)	Page 29
(beginning thought)	Ricky is terrified of dogs. I wonder if the dog bit him.
(thoughts)	Wow, He ended up on top of a fence he was so scared!
(questions)	I finally learned why Ricky is so scared of dogs. When he was little, he tried to pet a big dog and was attacked. A man saved him and thought he was dead. He got 63 stitches.
(closing thought)	What's hydrophobia? I think that's the big word for rabies. He had to get shots in his stomach. I bet the shots hurt. Poor Ricky's afraid of all dogs. I hope he can get over it.
(page I stopped)	p. 37

In the intermediate grades, students should keep a journal and write while they are reading. We call one popular format "Thoughts and Questions." While the students are reading, they simply jot down any thoughts and questions that arise. This is a great format for heightening the students' awareness of all the thinking and questioning they are doing while reading. See the top of page 122 for an example.

Date: March 15

Title: *Because of Winn Dixie*

Beginning Thought: I wonder how this book got its title. Winn Dixie is a grocery store.

Thoughts

Book seems to start off like a flashback.

First page mentions the store W-D.

I'm trying to picture this dog smiling.

Good descriptions–– like an old brown carpet…
  "he stunk. Bad."

Questions

Why does the girl refer to her dad as the "preacher"?

Will her dad let her keep the dog?

Ending Thought: Opal thinks this dog needs her. I would think it would be the other way around.

Fifth graders use the thoughts and questions model as they keep a reading journal. At left below, Mandy's journal shows a page from early in the school year when the teacher provided the structure. The second entry is without the support, but shows Mandy comfortably responding with her thoughts and questions.

Date 9/11/02

Title The Fellowship of the ring

Beginning Thought
If I were Frodo I would NOT want to be layed with the burden of the ring!

QUESTIONS	THOUGHTS
How far is Mordor?	This is taking a while for them to go.
What did Gandalf hear?	I like the name Sam Magee - it's funny
How did he get the nickname Fatty?	I love elves. They are interesting creatures.
What does fungal mean?	You'd think the Brickville Bagginses and the Baggins were related. But they hate each other
Where did Pippin go?	I think it's stupid to have a fire - Ringwraiths are out there.
Where did that song come from?	

Closing Thought In the movie Pippin didn't really accompany them till they were out of the Shire.
Page 163

3-5-03

I like the way you are answering big. four own questions.

Phoenix Rising   ch. 1

The reason I decided to read this book because I read another book by Karen Hesse, Letters from Rifka, and ranked 3rd favorite book.

1.
• The name Tyrus sounds like a god name.

• They might live in Japan, radiation.

• I bet her gran died, but then how did she get herself into the dieing room? - no

• It's strange. In all the books I read when a parent leaves you, you always want them. If my

2.
• Is Ripley Powers someones name? yes, funny name

• What happened? Why is her face covered with gause? - it's a radiation mask

• What if it's my birthday? It's in November.

• Where do they live?

• What was the accident that caused radiation!? Are they in World War 3?:

TEACHER to TEACHER

Students in our upper elementary classes enjoy "coding" their reading journals with symbols and abbreviations that help them classify the types of thinking they are doing as they read. For example, if a student likes the way the author crafted something, she might draw a hand in the margin of the journal and record the part from the book that she liked. In this way, the student "gives the author a hand." Another symbol many students use is the eyeball. They sketch an eyeball next to a quotation from the book that was especially vivid to remind them that this part helped them to visualize. Both of these symbols came out of students' own creativity, and there are many more like them. By coding their journals with their own meaningful symbols, students are able to take a look at their thinking process, and enjoy ownership in the process.

If some of your students have difficulty getting started with a response journal, provide prompts to give them ideas. Even with the use of prompts, make sure that you've modeled journal response using prompts. Take a look at the examples below.

WRITING ABOUT READING: POSSIBLE PROMPTS

- My favorite part…
- This book reminded me of…
- I made a prediction that…
- I wonder why…
- My favorite character was _____ because…
- I will recommend this book to other students because…
- I was confused when…
- Some words I'm not sure of are…
- I think the author wrote this book because…
- After reading this book I felt…

- A part in the book that disappointed me was…
- I was really surprised when…
- When I was reading this book, I felt…
- The part that I really pictured in my head was…
- I want to read other books by the same author because…
- I liked (or didn't like) the ending because…
- I like the way the author wrote…
- A writing technique I learned from this author that I want to try in my writing is…
- The theme of the story is…

Sharing

To culminate the Reading Workshop, readers gather to discuss their independent reading and to share with an audience. This sharing time provides students with opportunities to listen to and respect other readers. You can assess their oral language and listening skills, their ability to summarize and synthesize a text, and the depth of comments that they give to other readers.

We've found this to be a helpful opener for young readers: "What good reading work did you do today?" It is rewarding to hear responses such as: "I had to go back and reread because it didn't make sense." Or, "I figured out a really long word because I saw a little word in it."

This sharing time may provide a connection from the day's mini-lesson to the independent reading. For example, if the mini-lesson focused on the importance of the author's use of flashback, students can provide examples they found in their own reading.

It's also an opportunity for students to hear what other students do when they have trouble in reading. A student might share an example of how a strategy lesson helped as she encountered difficulty with her independent reading. "Today I kept getting confused with the word 'terrible' and 'trouble,' but then I remembered what you said about thinking what would make sense." Or, "Today when I was reading I got really confused, so I thought about what I already know about caterpillars and then I re-read the paragraph." During this time, you and your students can evaluate what they've done so that they can continue with what's been successful and abandon what hasn't been.

Remember, good sharing doesn't just happen. As with all other phases of the Reading Workshop, modeling, direct instruction, and constant feedback are your means to help make it happen.

You can demonstrate how to:

- 📖 share reactions to reading.

- 📖 elaborate on responses and provide evidence from the reading or from background knowledge.

- 📖 provide specific information to support student statements.

- 📖 use personal experience to support thinking.

- 📖 listen to others.

- 📖 ask questions of one another.

- 📖 ask questions and clear up confusion students have.

- 📖 respect one another in this dialogue.

Sharing is a time of closure, a coming together of a community of readers. And for you it is also another opportunity for assessment, part of every phase of the Reading Workshop and the topic of our next and final chapter.

TEACHER to TEACHER

Kids love to share. Many times though, what they want to say is quite off topic. In order to help younger students realize the difference between strong connections and off the subject connections, we introduced a hand puppet named "Oh No Oscar." During a few beginning read alouds and mini-lessons about connections, we read the book along with Oh No Oscar. During the reading, we would stop to make strong connections, but the puppet would pipe in with silly connections. By the end of the story, the kids were calling out, "Oh no, Oscar!" when we made a silly connection. As the days went by, students became adept at spotting an off the topic comment or superficial connection. Throughout the year, if an off topic comment is shared by a student, we simply need to make some quick reference to "Oh No Oscar" and we're back on track in our discussion!

CHAPTER 8

INFORMING INSTRUCTION:

Effective Assessment in the Reading Workshop

"Managing the workshop and keeping track of student progress is challenging but do-able. And the rewards of watching children enjoy reading make it well worthwhile."

—Jennifer Kinney, 3rd grade teacher

uthentic instruction in a Reading Workshop is the result of authentic assessment. Assessment occurs while students are involved in the job of real reading. A teacher's observing eyes and ears are always alert. Whether in an individual conversation about a book with one student or by listening in on a group discussion, she notes levels of comprehension and engagement, picks up on a student's level of accuracy and reading fluency, and watches out for what motivates a particular child. The written responses in a student's journal offer glimpses into a child's thinking and reflection processes and provide evidence of how well he or she is able to formulate responses. It's a daily job—gathering these assessments together, examining the data, and evaluating the performance of each student. Only when it's done does a teacher feel able to make instructional decisions. And as soon as that happens, the cycle starts again.

Matching Readers With Books

One of the first things to consider as you start a Reading Workshop is matching your readers with appropriately leveled books. You must know where your students are in their reading so that you can help them make appropriate book choices. Your goal is to get kids reading. If your school provides information about each student's reading level, use that as a guide to get started. You may need to spend time getting to know each child's level, especially those at each end of the continuum. Feel comfortable taking the time you need to get to know your readers.

Listening to Students' Reading

One of the easiest ways to assess your students is by listening to them read. You may want to use a graded oral reading passage. Or you might want to have various levels of books available to help you determine how the children handle the text. This type of "oral reading check-up" can help you assess reading level, fluency, types of miscues (errors), and comprehension. Before beginning, though, you'll want to inform your students about what you will be doing. They need to know that you will be taking notes as they read. Toward the end of your session, you may even want to share a few of your written comments with them.

Student Interviews

At the beginning of a school year, you gather information about your students. You learn of their attitudes toward reading, their book preferences, and their use of the reading process. It usually doesn't take long to get some sense of a child's home support and experiences with literacy. Simple interviews can help provide you with this sort of information. (See pages 127 and 128 for examples of one primary and one intermediate grade interview.)

Before interviewing your students about their attitudes toward reading, you may first want to share your own interests and feelings. You may even want to relate some of the feelings you had about reading while you were in school. Let your students know that you want to learn about them as readers so you can help them choose books they will love. Knowing this about them can help you plan to teach them what they need.

> ### TEACHER to TEACHER
> You might be wondering: "How can I keep track of my students if they aren't all using the same book or on the same page? How can I record conferences so that I know who I've met with and who I need to meet with next?"
>
> Developing a form for keeping track of conferences helps. The form on page 129 allows you to note students you will meet with on a daily basis for guided reading, those you need to touch base with regularly, and those stronger readers you can confer with a couple of times a week. It has space for recording topics for group lessons and a place for brief anecdotal notes. You can also use it to keep track of others who assist your students (reading specialist, learning specialist, volunteers).
>
> And as you get more experienced at conferencing, don't forget about sticky notes. Use these while working with a student; later stick them onto the student's record pages. Sticky notes are also helpful when you are first training yourself to keep reading conferences short. We've taken notes until the square note was full and then told ourselves it was time to move on. The sticky note proved to be a very reliable timer!

Revisiting the Reading Workshop: Management, Mini-Lessons, and Strategies • Scholastic Professional Books

Reading Interview
(Primary)

1. Do you like to read? _____   Why or why not? _____

_____

2. What do you do when something doesn't make sense? _____

_____

3. What do you do when you have trouble reading a word? _____

_____

4. How do pictures help you read? _____

_____

5. How do you feel when someone reads to you? _____

Who reads to you/how often? _____

_____

6. How do you feel when you are reading out loud? _____

_____

7. How often do you read at home? _____

8. What kinds of books do you like to read?

   ☐ picture books   ☐ chapter books   ☐ fantasy   ☐ nonfiction

   ☐ animal stories   ☐ other _____

9. Do you think reading is hard or easy for you? _____

Why? _____

10. Which face shows how you feel about reading?

   ☺   ☺   ☹

Reading Interview
(Intermediate)

1. Do you like to read? _____ Why or why not? _____

_____

2. What is your all-time favorite book? _____

_____

3. What are your favorite types of books to read? _____

_____

4. Do you have an author who you prefer? _____

Who is it? _____

Why do you prefer him/her? _____

_____

5. How often do you read? _____

6. Where do you like to read? _____

7. Do you like to be read to? _____ Why or why not? _____

_____

8. What do you think you do best in reading? _____

_____

9. What do you do when you have trouble reading a word? _____

_____

10. Do you recommend books to others? _____

11. Do you think you are a good reader? _____ Why or why not? _____

_____

12. What do you do when you don't understand something you are reading? _____

_____

13. What do you think would be a good goal for you in reading this year? _____

_____

Revisiting the Reading Workshop: Management, Mini-Lessons, and Strategies • Scholastic Professional Books

Week of _____

Mini-lesson topics _____

SKILL GROUPS PLANS

Date:
Topic:

Kids Attending:

Date:
Topic:

Kids Attending:

Date:
Topic:

Kids Attending:

Notes for next week's planning:

ANECDOTAL RECORDS

CLASS LIST

	M	T	W	T	F
1.					
2.					
3.					
4.					
5.					
6.					
7.					
8.					
9.					
10.					
11.					
12.					
13.					
14.					
15.					
16.					
17.					
18.					
19.					
20.					
21.					
22.					
23.					

Pulling Up a Chair: Procedures for Ongoing Observation of Students' Reading

In a successful Reading Workshop, assessment is ongoing and matches instruction. In fact, every phase of the Workshop provides numerous opportunities for just this kind of informal assessment. In this section, you'll find a comprehensive chart that spells out those opportunities and also a description of eight helpful observational tools that work particularly well in a Reading Workshop.

Opportunities for Observation and Assessment in a Reading Workshop

Teachers are often concerned about what should be assessed in a Reading Workshop. The chart on page 131 gives possible assessment opportunities in all Reading Workshop components.

Anecdotal Records

For the majority of reading conferences, you can take anecdotal records on labels, index cards, sticky notes, or record sheets and then add them to a notebook. Make note of behaviors you observe (pointing to words and whisper reading) as well as strategies used (use of picture clues, masking a word to find a known chunk, and re-reading).

While listening to a reading, focus on the following aspects:

- Reading behaviors
- Use of strategies
- Comprehension
- Fluency
- Plans for instruction

Take a look at the example of two index cards with anecdotal records of first graders (page 132). They illustrate how informal, and yet how thorough, a teacher's anecdotal records can be.

Keep the following in mind while you are taking anecdotal records:

- Be sure to date your notes.
  - This helps you keep track of how often you are conferring and the progress that occurs between conferences.
- Write brief but specific notes.
  - Rather than writing "Joshua did a better job today," write "Joshua self-corrected three errors: (like/look; want/what; isn't/is)."
  - Instead of writing "Kiera sounded better," state that "Kiera noticed all ending punctuation," or that "Kiera read dialogue appropriately. She is starting to sound like a reader."

OPPORTUNITIES FOR ASSESSMENT IN A READING WORKSHOP

Reading Workshop Component	What Occurs	Assessment Opportunity
Mini-Lesson	Teacher reads aloud: • models reading behaviors • teaches reading strategies • instructs in author's craft	Interest/participation Attentiveness/eye contact Response to questioning Demonstrated understanding of concepts
Independent Reading/ Conferring	Student selects books.	Strategies used to choose book Appropriate level of book Number of books read
	Student individually reads silently.	Engagement with text Amount of time on task Level of independence
	Student reads/discusses book with others (pairs, group).	Involvement in discussion with others Language used in discussing book Preparation done
	Student discusses book with teacher.	Retelling of reading Language used in discussing text Demonstrated understanding of reading Fluency Running record
Writing in Response to Reading	Student writes in response to reading: • Teacher directed • Personal response	Depth of understanding of reading Application of concepts Personal responses and reactions Ability to write in response to teacher direction Control over text conventions
Sharing	Students share insights from reading. Class responds and comments. Teacher intervenes, comments, and refocuses.	Confidence Willingness to share with an audience Oral language skills Listening skills Demonstrated ability to comprehend text Depth of comments given to other readers

1/10 Fluffy & Dinosaurs
✓✓✓✓✓   rdg w̄ exp
✓✓✓✓✓✓   good retelling/
✓ exclamation ✓ ✓   w̄ humor
exclaimed
✓✓✓✓✓✓✓✓
✓✓✓✓

2/5 Henry & Mudge
tenny
tennis

M just wagged = "That means
wagged his tail"
barked - parked - "they rhyme"

2/13 retold deer thru seasons - pointed out how to use
clue - snow melting   rdg to get wtg ideas
"sunshine tickled my nose"

2/20 Fox on Wheels - retelling

Alexandra

3/4 Bring Back my Gerbil
blurted - confused w̄
blurred
cloned? - explained
rdg w̄ expression

3/12 Pandas
good background
knowledge
shared w̄ Alex F who
saw Pandas

3/20 Fantastic Frogs
used index to choose
frogs to rd
about

3/25 Owls
shared "eagle owls" - rd
why called " "

1/8 Brought bk to me that Tony said was too easy. Asked if he
could read it (Don't Worry) - knows his level - just rt bk
for him

1/9 Two Crazy Pigs - noticed picture didn't make sense

1/10 Danny & the Dinosaur - partner rdg w̄ Chase
noticed 'stared' - not started

1/23 Arthur's Eyes - said his friends are jealous of his glasses
understand "4 eyes"
helped w̄ 'clearer' & 'decided'

2/5 Harry & Terrible Whatzit   wizard   - helped decode   not —
whatzit   noticed

couldn't make connections bec a monster

2/6 Golly Sisters Go West   ready   fluent / rds dialogue
ready   w̄ exp.

2/18 Waterhole - re-rd several times, likes nf.
comfortable level / discussed probs if
animals go to zoos

Joel

◆ Instead of noting that "Kate's book was too hard," note that "Kate made five errors in the first two sentences; helped her find a better choice on same topic."

◆ Provide specifics when assessing comprehension.
"Chris was able to retell using all story elements."
"Tony still can't determine the setting in his story. Find books where it is more obvious."
"Nijel can retell facts and specific details from his book about snakes. Wants more books on snakes."

📖 Use your anecdotal records to hold students accountable for previous instruction. For example, if you noticed at the last two conferences that Caren was choosing books that were too easy, then you will check at the next conference to make sure that she has chosen an appropriate book.

📖 While you take these notes, think about what students need and make plans for future instruction. Think about forming small flexible groups that are based on needs.

Observational Checklists

Checklists provide quick and easy assessment. They don't take much time to prepare and can be individualized for your needs. With young children, you may want to assess level of engagement during your read aloud time. Develop a checklist that has the attributes you are evaluating: eye contact, engagement, listening posture, retelling ability. If you are working with intermediate students, you may want to assess preparedness for a story chat. Develop a checklist to meet those needs: prepared for discussion, has book and journal, asks questions of others, responds to others' questions. See the examples of checklists on pages 134 and 135.

Whether through direct observation of a student's reading or through careful analysis of a child's written reflection, we are always engaged in informal assessment during the Reading Workshop.

Story Chat Checklist

STUDENT	Assignment completed	Prepared with materials (book & journal)	Contributes to group discussion	Listens to and asks questions of others	Responds to others' questions	Uses background knowledge	Makes appropriate connections	Provides supportive evidence

Revisiting the Reading Workshop: Management, Mini-Lessons, and Strategies • Scholastic Professional Books

Week of _____

Independent Reading Checklist

STUDENT	Spends majority of time reading	Reads silently	Makes appropriate book choices	Chooses from a variety of genres	Discusses books with others	Provides written response to literature	Logs books read	Completes books

Running Records

A running record is a method that allows teachers to code and analyze a student's oral reading (Clay, 1993). Running records are usually taken on unfamiliar material. All you need to have available is a piece of paper since no prepared written script is necessary. This is especially important in a Reading Workshop because you have students reading various books, and you need to record how each is interacting with a particular text selection. A running record helps you determine how the child handles text, especially as he or she encounters difficulty. During a conference, you just pull up a chair, listen in as the child reads, and code the reading behaviors on a piece of paper. Every word that is read accurately is coded with a √. There are codes for other miscues such as self-corrections, repetitions, substitutions, insertions, omissions, and "tolds" (where the student is told the word). Take a look at the following text and the way it is coded (*Fox and Friends* by Edward Marshall).

By looking over the running record, you can determine the type of errors made and judge if the text was too easy or difficult. Running records also provide you with valuable information for planning individual or group instruction.

If you are unfamiliar with running records, we recommend that you read Marie Clay's book, *An Observation Survey of Early Literacy Achievement* (1993). It is very thorough in explaining how to take running records in addition to coding and scoring them. Another practical source is *Taking Running Records* by May Shea (2000).

SAMPLE RUNNING RECORD

"Last one in the pool
is a monkey's uncle!" said Dexter.
And everyone ran for the pool.
Soon everyone was having a lot of fun.
"This is wild!" said Fox.
And everyone agreed.

√ √ √ √ √	(accurate reading)
√ √ <u>monkey</u> —— √ √ monkey's uncle	(substitution) (omission)
√ <u>everybody</u> √ √ √ <u>swimming</u> √ everyone ——	(substitution) (insertion)
√R <u>everybody</u> /sc √ √ √ √ √ √ everyone	(repetition) (self-correction)
√ √ √ √	(accurate reading)
√ √ <u>ag ag</u> /T agreed	(told)

Informal Error Analysis

After listening in on a child's reading and analyzing the types of errors made, it's helpful to look for a pattern. Errors usually fall into three categories:

📖 **Graphophonics: the visual or letter-sound system of language ("Does it look right?")**
A child may read "Dad drove his <u>car</u> to work" instead of "Dad drove his <u>truck</u> to work." The word makes sense, but the child did not pay close attention to the way the word looked.

📖 **Syntax: the grammar or structure of the language ("Does it sound right?")**
When a child reads "You must took care of your dog" instead of "You must take care of your dog," it is grammatically incorrect and doesn't sound right.

📖 **Semantics: the meaning system of language ("Does it make sense?")**
If a child reads "The boy rode the <u>house</u> at Grandpa's farm" instead of "The boy rode the <u>horse</u> at Grandpa's farm," the child used visual clues to attempt to figure out the word, but didn't use meaning.

Although running records are usually done with younger readers, you can use this same approach with older students. Because older readers are usually so much more fluent, you may have a hard time recording every accurate word. In this case, it's fine to simply indicate the errors made. The important part comes in when you analyze their reading. You'll want to ask yourself questions such as:

📖 Is there a pattern to the errors?

📖 Do the errors interrupt the meaning?

📖 Is the student self-correcting?

📖 Does he seem to understand what he is reading?

📖 Is the child fluent?

📖 Is he whisper reading during "silent" reading?

By looking at the errors and reading behaviors, you can decide what skills and strategies need further instruction.

Oral Retellings

We spend a lot of time with our students on oral retellings. As we pull up alongside a child, we ask him or her to stop and tell us what is going on in the book. It's amazing how much information you can glean by this simple process.

Fiction

When a child is reading a piece of fiction, you should determine if he or she has a sense of the story and can identify the characters, the setting, and the plot. Often it is hard for students to recognize a problem that may have occurred in the story. It is much easier for them to relate events, although not necessarily in sequence. Some students relate every single event they can think of. Others have difficulty remembering very much at all. They seem to be concentrating so hard on decoding that they aren't thinking about what they are reading. As you listen in on a retelling, ask questions like the following:

Characters— Can you tell me who the main character is?
Who are some of the other important characters in this story?

Setting— Have you figured out where the story takes place?
What about when it takes place?

Problem— What is the problem in the story?

Events— Can you tell me the main events? Try to tell them to me in the order in which
they happened.

Resolution— How is the problem solved in your story?

Ending— How does the author end the story? What do you think of the ending?

Nonfiction

If the child is reading a nonfiction piece, the retelling will be quite different. Check to see
what the child has learned from the book. Can he summarize the main ideas and identify any
subtopics? Does he seem to understand key vocabulary? Does he use any previous knowledge
in understanding new material? You may want to use questions like the following in
nonfiction retellings:

- Can you summarize the main idea of what you've read?

- What are some of the other topics or ideas that were in your reading?

- What are some things you knew about the topic before you started reading? How has that
background knowledge helped you?

- What new vocabulary or terms did you learn?

- Can you make any connections between the text and yourself?

- Tell me the events (or steps) in order.

- What is something you learned from what you just read?

Written Retellings

With older students, ask for a written retelling of a story or chapter they have read. Be sure to
make your expectations clear. The key here is modeling: if you expect your students to write a
summary of a chapter in a chapter book, model how to write a summary. Show them what
you want included and explain that you want a good summary, but not one that is too
lengthy.

Reading Logs

Requiring your students to keep logs of the books they read is also a good idea. When
students are responsible for logging the title, author, number of pages read, and (for older
students) genre, not only are they learning to keep records, but *you* are gaining valuable
information for assessment purposes. You can quickly discern how many books have been
read, the types of books read, how long it takes a child to finish a book, and which books
have been abandoned. Reading logs are also a good springboard for discussions with parents
and students.

Journal Responses

Thoughtful readers are reflective readers. Expect all of your students to respond to their reading. However, what you can expect at the intermediate level is different from what you expect at the primary level. All written responses provide a wealth of information for assessment. From student response, you can determine the level of understanding of the reading or of the mini-lesson. You can also assess if a student is able to follow directions. And you can evaluate how complete the journal is and whether it follows the conventions of writing.

Journals provide you with tangible material to discuss with a student. During a conference, point out how pleased you are to see the figurative language the student noted after a mini-lesson on similes and metaphors. Let the student know that you noticed use of the strategies on questioning and making connections in his or her journal entries. Having a dialogue with a student about his or her journal shows that you value the student's response and reflection.

Evaluating Progress

Although effective teachers evaluate the progress of each student on a daily basis, they also realize that grades must somehow be assigned. You need to make sure your students and their parents are aware of your expectations: the student's role during the Reading Workshop, the number of books expected to be read, the importance of take-home reading, the written response in their journal, and their role in record keeping.

Reading conferences benefit both student and teacher. The student receives one-on-one reading instruction while the teacher gains insight into how the reader is managing the text.

Semester End Reading Inventory

One of the greatest strengths of the Reading Workshop is the built-in flexibility that allows the teacher to tailor instruction for individual needs. However, it's quite difficult to translate individual activities into generic report card grades. We developed the Semester End Reading Inventory out of the need to determine such grades. You can adapt this inventory for any grade and for any objectives. The idea is to keep the inventory quite open ended, but still specific enough so that the information you want is given back to you. By using a Semester End Reading Inventory you'll have something on paper, something to look at and consider when it comes to putting grades on report cards. It's also a great way to find out who needs help with what skill when planning for the next semester. The example at the top of page 140 illustrates a completed Inventory. In the Appendices, pages 158–159, we provide a blank form for your own use.

Name Evan   Date_____

End Semester Reading Inventory

Knowing what to read...

How do you select a "just right" book? How do you know it is a "just right book"? Can you give an example of a "just right book"?

you open to a page and then you read it, Then do a five finger test. I, Haudini is a just right book for me.

Knowing how to read...

How many reading strategies can you think of? Can you tell how you use each one?

Strategy name...	How I can use it...
Pridicting	I can predict what is going to happen.
Visoulizeation	I put a picture in my head.
Questioning	I can ask myself question.
Self-montering.	I can help myself if I don't understand something

Knowing what to look for...

How many story elements can you list?

setting, cange, problem, plot, time, a charictors.

What are some things that good authors do in their writing?

They rerite, they words that put realy, realy good pictures in your head.

What was your favorite read-aloud this year? Tell why you liked it.

Stikeen because it was so exiting.

What was the best book you read to yourself? Tell why you liked it.

The Magic Tree House Books because...

How have you become a better reader?

Yes! Alot better!

What is one goal for yourself as a reader?

To read harder and longer books.

Rubrics

A rubric is a scoring device that is based on specific performance criteria for key elements you want to assess. It is perfect for the Reading Workshop because it allows you to determine the performance standards for reading behaviors in the Workshop. By sharing these standards with your students up front, you can show them how you will assess their participation in mini-lessons, their engagement during independent reading, and their journaling efforts. Creating rubrics that meet your needs allows you to interpret and assign a score to a student's performance.

Most rubrics are set up with **key elements** and **criteria**. Look at the filled-in rubric at right (or the same blank rubric on page 141); notice that "Mini-Lesson," "Reading/Conferring," "Journaling," and "Take Home Reading" are the key elements. Within each

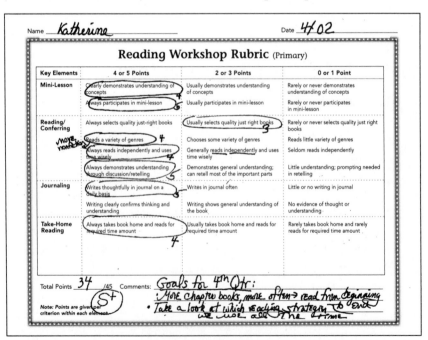

Name _____

Date _____

Reading Workshop Rubric (Primary)

Key Elements	4 or 5 Points	2 or 3 Points	0 or 1 Point
Mini-Lesson	Clearly demonstrates understanding of concepts	Usually demonstrates understanding of concepts	Rarely or never demonstrates understanding of concepts
	Always participates in mini-lesson	Usually participates in mini-lesson	Rarely or never participates in mini-lesson
Reading/ Conferring	Always selects quality just-right books	Usually selects quality just right books	Rarely or never selects quality just right books
	Reads a variety of genres	Chooses some variety of genres	Reads little variety of genres
	Always reads independently and uses time wisely	Generally reads independently and uses time wisely	Seldom reads independently
	Always demonstrates understanding through discussion/retelling	Demonstrates general understanding; can retell most of the important parts	Little understanding; prompting needed in retelling
Journaling	Writes thoughtfully in journal on a daily basis	Writes in journal often	Little or no writing in journal
	Writing clearly confirms thinking and understanding	Writing shows general understanding of the book	No evidence of thought or understanding
Take-Home Reading	Always takes book home and reads for required time amount	Usually takes book home and reads for required time amount	Rarely takes book home and rarely reads for required time amount

Total Points _____ /45   Comments: _____

_____

_____

***Note:** Points are given per criterion within each element.*

Reading Workshop Rubric (Intermediate)

Key Elements	5 Points	4 Points	3 Points	2 Points
Mini-Lesson	Consistently demonstrates understanding of concepts	Usually demonstrates understanding of concepts	Sometimes demonstrates understanding of concepts	Rarely or never demonstrates understanding of concepts
	Always participates in mini-lesson	Usually participates in mini-lesson	Sometimes participates in mini-lesson	Rarely or never participates in mini-lesson
Reading/ Conferring	Consistently selects quality books at appropriate level	Usually selects books at appropriate level	Sometimes selects books at appropriate level	Has difficulty choosing books at appropriate level
	Consistently identifies the genre of the book he/she is reading	Usually identifies the genre of the book he/she is reading	Sometimes identifies the genre of the book he/she is reading	Never identifies the genre of the book he/she is reading
	Consistently reads independently and uses time wisely	Usually reads independently and uses time wisely	Sometimes reads independently and uses time wisely	Rarely reads independently
	Demonstrates clear understanding through discussion/retelling	Demonstrates general understanding; can retell most of the important points	Inconsistently demonstrates understanding; can retell some of the important points	Demonstrates little understanding; prompting needed in retelling
	Consistently uses reading strategies	Usually uses reading strategies	Sometimes uses reading strategies	Rarely uses reading strategies
	Consistently completes books	Usually completes books	Often abandons books	Usually abandons books
Journaling	Consistently completes journal when assigned	Usually completes journal when assigned	Sometimes completes journal when assigned	Rarely or never completes journal when assigned
	Consistently writes quality entries	Usually writes quality entries	Sometimes writes quality entries	Rarely writes quality entries
Take-Home Reading	Consistently reads for the required amount of time; completes home reading log	Usually reads for the required amount of time and completes home reading log	Sometimes reads for the required amount of time and completes home reading log	Rarely reads for the required amount of time or completes home reading log

Total Points _____ /55   Comments:

Note: Points are given per criterion within each element.

Reading Journal Assessment

	4–5 Points	2–3 Points	0–1 Point
Comprehension	Written response demonstrates clear understanding of reading	Written response demonstrates a general understanding of reading	Written response is vague and unclear.
Application of Mini-Lesson/ Instruction	Consistently applies concepts of mini-lessons/instruction	Usually applies concepts of mini-lessons/instruction	Unable to apply concepts of mini-lesson/instruction
Completeness	Journal consistently done and turned in on time	Journal usually done and turned in on time	Journal not turned in on time
	Always includes dates, book title(s), genre, pages read.	Usually includes dates, book title(s), genre, pages read.	Rarely or never complete.
Personal Response	Personally reacts to and responds to texts	Some personal response and reaction	Little or no personal response or reaction
Writing Conventions	Demonstrates proper conventions; neat and legible	Demonstrates some writing conventions; readable	Inconsistent use of writing conventions; illegible

Total Points _____ /30   Comments: _____

_____

_____

_____

_____

Note: *Points are given per criterion within each element.*

element are specific criteria. Teachers evaluate the criteria and assign each a point value from three possible point value categories. Both the Reading Journal Assessment rubric (see page 143), and the Reading Journal Rubric (see below), while focused specifically on journal entry writing, follow the same rubric format.

Reading Journal Rubric

Name *Katherine*   Date *4/16/02*

	4 or 5 points	2 or 3 points	0 or 1 point
Use of details from the reading	Uses many details that prove a book was read and understood	Uses some details that show some reading and understanding was done	Use few or no details
Use of independent thought	Clearly proves that student is thinking about the reading	Some proof that student is thinking about the reading	No proof of any independent thought
Punctuation	Always has correct punctuation in sentences	Usually has correct punctuation in sentences	Rarely has correct punctuation in sentences
Spelling	Most words are spelled correctly; many attempts made to fix errors	Most words are spelled correctly; few attempts made to fix errors	Few words are spelled correctly
Neatness and Effort	Clear proof that the student cares about the quality of the work	Some proof that care has been given to the writing	Little proof that care has been given to the writing

Total ___17___ points/ 25 points   Comments:

Keep up your strong thoughts — just tell me more about the story!

Rubrics Inform Instruction

Rubrics can help inform your teaching. By looking at the highest criteria, you can set the standard for your teaching as well as goals for your students. (See the "Good Assessment" box on page 147 for recommendations about how to establish sound goals for individual students.) Further, it is essential to share rubrics with the class so students are explicitly aware of your standards, of how they will be held accountable, and of what they need to do to reach the next level of performance. Notice in the following sample conference how rubrics are used to inform students of their progress and move them on to the next level.

RUBRIC CONFERENCE

Teacher: Hi, Katherine. Today, instead of reading your book with you, I'd thought we'd take the time to do our rubric conference before report cards come out again. Do you remember what we do in a rubric conference?

Student: Yes, we talk about what I've done in the past and we talk about a grade for Reading.

T: Yes, that's right. Let's start with the first part of the Workshop and that's the mini-lesson. Tell me, do you feel as if you are always participating and being a strong listener when we meet for mini-lessons?

S: Usually. Sometimes I have to remember not to talk to Michael, though.

T: Yes, I agree. But, when I look at my checklist here, I notice that the comments you make are always on the topic and that you often share your thoughts with us during mini-lesson time. I'm very pleased with your participation. I'm going to give you 5 points. So keep up the great work. Now, let's take a look at your mini-lesson main ideas. Does what you write every day prove that you are learning from the mini-lesson?

S: I think sometimes. Sometimes I forget to write in complete sentences and when I go back to review, I forget what I was trying to say the main idea was.

T: Yes, I can see that in your notes. But I still see that you almost always include the key words of our mini-lesson. I'll give you four points. Let's try and make it five points next time by remembering to write your mini-lesson main ideas in complete sentences. Okay? Now let's talk about your actual reading. Let's look in your reading log at what you have been reading.

(Student shares reading log and comments on the book selection.)

T: Let me tell you what I notice. I see some really great chapter books here, but only listed for one or two days. That tells me that you are not finishing them. I also see lots and lots of picture books. Picture books are great, but I know you are a very strong reader and I don't think the picture books you are choosing are exercising your reading muscles. I'd really like to see you choose more just right books and read those books to the very end.

S: Yeah, sometimes I forget to bring my book home and then I just forget I was even reading it. And I really love the stories in picture books, so I think that's why I keep going back.

T: Picture books do have great stories, but I guarantee you'll find some excellent stories in chapter books as well. After we're done with the rubric, I'll help you find a couple of really good ones to get that started. In fact, let's make that one of your goals for the next quarter...more chapter books, especially more chapter books that you finish. Deal?

S: Deal. I think I do the next two things really well. I read all different kinds of books and I always understand what I'm reading.

T: I agree. You've got lots of different genres here. But I'd still like to see you spend a little more time with non-fiction. And I want you to think about what you said when we were talking about the mini-lesson, how you sometimes talk to Michael. I think you do that during book nooks, too. So I'm going to give you four points for using all the time wisely.

S: I guess you're right. Maybe I could read one of those chapter books with Michael?

T: That sounds like a plan to me! Now, let's take a look at your journal.

(Student's journal is neat, complete with beginning thoughts, thoughts and questions throughout the day's reading, and a pretty strong ending thought.)

T: Can you tell me a little about your journal?

S: I like to do the journal. I like writing my predictions down so I can see if I guessed right at the end. I like asking questions while I read. Sometimes that makes me feel like I'm right in the book.

T: I like your journal too. I especially like how you tell me a little about what is happening and a little about what you are thinking. That's a good balance. Please keep it up.

S: I know I will do that.

T: Good. The last thing we need to talk about is take-home reading. You turned in 8 out of 9 weekly take-home logs. I'll give four points for that. Let's see if you can get all 9 in next time.

S: I will. I still don't know what happened to that other one.

T: Okay. We're done. Can you tell me what goal we said you were going to work on?

S: Yeah, I am going to read more chapter books and finish them.

T: Exactly. Can you record that goal in your journal right now so that you don't forget? Also, since you'll be reading some longer and maybe even harder texts, I want you to think about the reading strategies you are using. Are you visualizing, asking questions, making connections? These are the things I'll be talking about with you when we conference, so I want you to be thinking about them.

S: Okay. So, I'll write that, too: "What strategies am I using?"

T: Katherine, you've done a great job. I'm very proud. And, I know next quarter will be even better! Thank you.

Rubrics Help You to Assign Grades in a Reading Workshop

Teachers in the intermediate grades frequently ask: "How do I assign letter grades in reading when my students are participating in a Reading Workshop?" First of all, keep in mind that you will know more about your readers and have more data on your students than you ever did in the past.

The grade you give a student should reflect a total picture of that student in the Reading Workshop. It should take into account the student's involvement in the mini-lesson as well as what the student has done during independent reading time. Student conferences provide you with valuable information about how the student handles text and constructs meaning during reading. And the student's writing is an important piece that can provide documentation. You might even consider the home-school connection if you require students to read at home nightly. Using a rubric will help you assess students in all parts of the Reading Workshop. It will also provide you with a way to assign point values to the different Workshop components.

Communication

It is important to keep parents informed of your assessment procedures. A letter of explanation can provide some clarification. This is helpful especially if parents have become familiar with a different assessment process in previous years. It will make for smooth parent-teacher conferences in the future.

For our parent conferences, we developed the Reading Conference Quarterly Notes (see page 147), modeled after a KWL chart. Throughout the quarter, we keep track of what the student knows and add what he needs to know. By the end of the quarter we (parent and teacher) decide how we are going to get the child where he needs to go next.

Rubrics and anecdotal records are essential at these conferences. At the conference, you can help parents focus on a child's strengths or weaknesses and show them clearly what the child needs to do to reach the next performance level. When the student's personal goals are recorded on an individual reading rubric or a KWL chart, they are vastly more informative than a letter or number grade could ever be.

Reading Conference Quarterly Notes

Name _Jonathan_   Date _11/00_

What he/she KNOW?	What does he/she NEED TO KNOW?	How can WE go about this?
decoding skills are coming along demonstrated ability to pick "just right" books for himself reading must make sense— he's able to retell simple stories with solid accuracy	more sight recognition of blends esp. ch, cl Like to see more re-reading as he fixes up mistakes) We'll work more with long and short vowels... this will result in faster decoding	Continue to read with and to Jonathan everyday! Encourage him to write a little about what he's reading Use some of the following prompts when reading with him ·Why did you stop? ·Check it. Does it look or sound right to you? ·What could you do to help yourself?

GOOD ASSESSMENT HELPS STUDENTS MAKE PROGRESS

The primary purpose of assessing students is to help them move forward in their learning. Be clear as you guide them toward their next steps. Whether you are doing a full evaluation conference or are just leaving the reader with some good advice before you move on to another conference, it's a good idea to set one or two goals for each child. And, by all means, be sure each child knows what his or her individual goals are. While the following list of possible goals is by no means exhaustive, it gives you a starting point for setting individual goals in your classroom.

◆ Choose more just right books that match true reading ability.

◆ Read more of a certain genre.

◆ Stop reading when something doesn't make sense. Ask a question, reread, or use a context clue.

◆ Practice reading at home every night.

◆ Stop yourself after every other page or so and remind yourself what is happening in the story. If you aren't sure, go back and reread!

◆ Think about what you already know about a topic before diving into the book.

◆ Use all of your reading time carefully and thoughtfully.

◆ Try to pick up your reading pace. If you read 6 pages yesterday, can you read 8 today?

◆ When you read out loud, make your reading sound like a friend is talking to you.

◆ Think about the book's big picture: what lesson could you learn, why did the author write the book?

A Final Thought...

AS WE REFLECT ON THE PRECEDING PAGES, WE HOPE THAT WE have made it clear that the Reading Workshop works because it is an investment. Teachers invest time and energy in creating the environment, preparing the instruction, and providing the guidance. Students invest time and energy in learning about themselves as thinkers and readers, making decisions about their own literate lives, and taking responsibility for what they need to know next.

In this day of standards-based education, we hear all too often that there's just not enough time to get things done in the classroom. It's important that you make time for those things that really matter. Things like reading, and reading well. Things like thinking, thinking for oneself, and thinking about others. Time does matter. The Reading Workshop helps us to give our students as much time as possible for these worthwhile endeavors.

We urge you now to take back this needed time. Go and put that "Shhh! We're reading" sign on your own classroom door. Take your students by their hands and help them to discover for themselves all the magic behind those printed words. We promise you, this is the good part. It's your turn now, go read with them.

Recommended Children's Literature for Your Reading Workshop

Aesop. *City Mouse and Country Mouse*. New York: Scholastic, 1970.

Ahlberg, Janet, and Allen Ahlberg. *Each Peach Pear Plum*. New York: Viking Press, 1978.

Babbitt, Natalie. *Tuck Everlasting*. New York: Farrar, Straus & Giroux, 1975.

Bahr, Mary. *The Memory Box*. Morton Grove, IL: Albert Whitman & Co., 1992.

Ballard, Robert D. *Finding the Titanic*. New York: Cartwheel Books, 1993.

Bang, Molly. *Goose*. New York: Blue Sky Press, 1996.

Baylor, Byrd. *The Way to Start a Day*. New York: Simon & Schuster, 1978.

Bedard, Michael. *Emily*. New York: Doubleday, 1992.

Beil, Karen Magnuson. *Grandma According to Me*. New York: Doubleday Books for Young Readers, 1992.

Bertram, Debbie and Susan Bloom. *The Best Place to Read*. New York: Random House, 2003.

Bloom, Becky. *Wolf!* New York: Orchard Books, 1999.

Blume, Judy. *The Pain and the Great One*. New York: Bantam Doubleday Dell, 1974.

Bradby, Marie. *More Than Anything Else*. New York: Orchard Books, 1995.

Brett, Jan. *The Mitten*. New York: G.P. Putnam's Sons, 1989.

Briggs, Raymond. *Jim and the Beanstalk*. New York: Sandcastle Books, 1970.

Brinckloe, Julie. *Fireflies*. New York: Macmillan, 1985.

Brown, Margaret Wise. *The Runaway Bunny*. New York: HarperCollins, 1970.

Brown, Ruth. *A Dark, Dark Tale*. New York: Dial Books for Young Readers, 1991.

Bunting, Eve. *Fly Away Home*. Boston: Clarion Books, 1991.

Bunting, Eve. *Memory String*. New York: Clarion Books, 2000.

Bunting, Eve. *On Call Back Mountain*. New York: Blue Sky Press, 1997.

Bunting, Eve. *Smoky Night*. San Diego: Harcourt Brace, 1995.

Bunting, Eve. *Swan in Love*. New York: Atheneum Books, 2000.

Bunting, Eve. *Train to Somewhere*. New York: Clarion Books, 1996.

Bunting, Eve. *The Wall*. New York: Clarion Books, 1990.

Bunting, Eve. *The Wednesday Surprise*. New York: Clarion Books, 1989.

Bushnell, Jack. *Sky Dancer*. New York: Lothrop, Lee & Shepard Books, 1996.

Byars, Betsy. *The Pinballs*. New York: HarperCollins, 1977.

Calhoun, Mary. *Hot-Air Henry*. New York: Morrow Junior Books, 1981.

Cameron, Polly. *I Can't Said the Ant*. New York: Putnam, 1961.

Cannon, Janell. *Stellaluna*. San Diego: Harcourt Brace, 1993.

Cannon, Janell. *Verdi*. San Diego: Harcourt Brace, 1997.

Carle, Eric. *Pancakes, Pancakes*. New York: Scholastic, 1990.

Carle, Eric. *The Tiny Seed*. New York: Simon & Schuster, 1991.

Carlstrom, Nancy White. *Jesse Bear, What Will You Wear?* New York: Macmillan, 1986.

Carlstrom, Nancy White. *The Snow Speaks*. Boston: Little, Brown & Co., 1992.

Carlstrom, Nancy White. *Where Does the Night Hide?* New York: Macmillan, 1990.

Catalanotto, Peter. *Mr. Mumble*. New York: Orchard Books, 1990.

Catling, Patrick Skene. *The Chocolate Touch*. New York: William Morrow & Co., 1952.

Chall, Marsha Wilson. *Bonaparte*. New York: DK Publishing, 2000.

Chall, Marsha Wilson. *Up North at the Cabin*. New York: Lothrop, Lee & Shepard, 1992.

Charlip, Remy. *Why I Will Never, Ever, Ever, Ever Have Enough Time to Read This Book*. Berkeley: Tricycle Press, 2000.

Cherry, Lynne. *Great Kapok Tree*. New York: Harcourt Brace, 1990.

Chesworth, Michael. *Archibald Frisby*. New York: Farrar, Straus & Giroux, 1994.

Chorao, Kay. *Pig and Crow*. New York: Henry Holt, 2000.

Cleary, Beverly. *Ramona Forever*. New York: William Morrow & Co., 1984.

Climo, Shirley. *Egyptian Cinderella*. New York: HarperCollins, 1989.

Cooney, Barbara. *Eleanor*. New York: Viking Penguin, 1996.

Cooney, Barbara. *Miss Rumphius*. New York: Puffin, 1982.

Cooper, Melrose. *Gettin' Through Thursday*. New York: Lee & Low, 1998.

Curtis, Jamie Lee. *Where Do Balloons Go?* New York: HarperCollins, 2000.

Danneberg, Julie. *First Day Jitters*. Watertown, MA: Charlesbridge, 2000.

Day, Alexandra. *Carl Makes a Scrapbook*. New York: Farrar, Straus & Giroux, 1994.

Deedy, Carmen, Agra. *The Library Dragon*. Atlanta: Peachtree Publishers, 1994.

DiCamillo, Kate. *Because of Winn Dixie*. Cambridge, MA: Candlewick Press, 2000.

Fanelli, Sara. *My Map Book*. New York: HarperCollins, 1995.

Fenner, Carol. *Yolanda's Genius*. New York: Simon & Schuster, 1995.

Fitzpatrick, Marie-Louise. *Lizzy and Skunk*. New York: Dorling Kindersley, 2000.

Finchler, Judy. *Miss Malarkey Doesn't Live in Room 10*. New York: Walker & Co., 1995.

Fleming, Denise. *In the Small, Small Pond*. New York: Henry Holt, 1993.

Fleming, Denise. *In the Tall, Tall Grass*. New York: Henry Holt, 1991.

Fleming, Virginia. *Be Good to Eddie Lee*. New York: Philomel Books, 1993.

Flournoy, Valerie. *The Patchwork Quilt*. New York: Dial Books for Young Readers, 1985.

Fox, Mem. *Koala Lou*. San Diego: Harcourt Brace Jovanovich, 1989.

Fox, Mem. *Wilfrid Gordon McDonald Partridge*. Brooklyn: Kane/Miller Book Publishers, 1985.

Fraustino, Lisa Rowe. *The Hickory Chair*. New York: Scholastic, 2001.

Friedman, Ina R. *How My Parents Learned to Eat*. Boston: Houghton Mifflin, 1984.

Galdone, Paul. *The Gingerbread Boy*. New York: Clarion Books, 1975.

Galdone, Paul. *The Little Red Hen*. New York: Clarion Books, 1973.

Gardiner, John Reynolds. *Stone Fox*. New York: HarperCollins, 1980.

George, Jean Craighead. *Julie of the Wolves*. New York: HarperCollins, 1972.

Gilbert, Suzie. *Hawk Hill*. San Francisco: Chronicle Books, 1996.

Gliori, Debi. *The Snow Lambs*. New York: Scholastic, 1996.

Golenbock, Peter. *Teammates*. San Diego: Harcourt Brace Jovanovich, 1990.

Gomi. *The Crocodile and the Dentist*. Brookfield, CT: Millbrook Press, 1984.

Goodall, Jane. *Dr. White*. New York: North-South Books, 1999.

Goodall, Jane. *The Eagle and the Wren*. New York: North-South Books, 2000.

Gray, Libba Moore. *Dear Willie Rudd*. New York: Simon & Schuster, 1993.

Gray, Libba Moore. *My Mama Had a Dancing Heart*. New York: Orchard Books, 1995.

Greenfield, Eloise. *Grandpa's Face*. New York: The Putnam & Grosset Group, 1988.

Grossman, Bill. *My Little Sister Ate One Hare*. New York: Crown Publishers, 1996.

Hall, Donald. *I Am the Dog; I Am the Cat*. New York: Dial Books,1994.

Hall, Donald. *Ox-Cart Man*. New York: Viking Penguin, 1979.

Haseley, Dennis. *A Story for Bear*. San Diego: Harcourt, 2002.

Heller, Ruth. *Chickens Aren't the Only Ones*. New York: Grosset & Dunlap, 1981.

Heller, Ruth. *Reason for a Flower*. New York: Putnam Publishing Group, 1983.

Henkes, Kevin. *Chester's Way*. New York: Viking Penguin, 1988.

Henkes, Kevin. *Chrysanthemum*. New York: Greenwillow Books, 1991.

Henkes, Kevin. *Grandpa and Bo*. New York: Greenwillow Books, 2002.

Henkes, Kevin. *Lily's Purple Plastic Purse*. New York: Greenwillow Books, 1996.

Henkes, Kevin. *Wemberley Worried*. New York: Greenwillow Books, 2000.

Hesse, Karen. *Letters from Rifka*. New York: Puffin, 1992.

Hesse, Karen. *Phoenix Rising*. New York: Henry Holt, 1994.

Hest, Amy. *When Jessie Came Across the Sea*. Cambridge, MA: Candlewick, 1997.

Hoban, Russell. *Bedtime for Frances*. New York: HarperCollins, 1960.

Hoffman, Mary. *Amazing Grace*. New York: Dial Books for Young Readers, 1991.

Hoose, Philip, and Hannah Hoose. *Hey, Little Ant*. Berkeley: Tricycle Press, 1998.

Hopping, Lorraine Jean. *Earthquake!* New York: Scholastic, 2002.

Howard, Arthur. *When I Was Five*. San Diego: Harcourt Brace, 1996.

Huck, Charlotte (retold by). *Princess Furball*. New York: Greenwillow Books, 1989.

Hunter, Sally. *Humphrey's Corner*. New York: Henry Holt, 1999.

Inkpen, Deborah. *Harriet*. Hauppauge, NY: Barron's, 1998.

James, Simon. *Dear Mr. Blueberry*. New York: McElderry Books, 1991.

Jenkins, Steve. *The Top of the World: Climbing Mt. Everest*. Boston: Houghton Mifflin, 1999.

Johnson, Angela. *The Leaving Morning*. New York: Orchard Books, 1992.

Johnson, Paul Brett and Celeste Lewis. *Lost*. New York: Orchard Books, 1996.

Johnston, Tony. *Amber on the Mountain*. New York: Penguin, 1994.

Joosse, Barbara M. *I Love You the Purplest*. San Francisco: Chronicle Books, 1996.

Kellogg, Steven. *Jack and the Beanstalk*. New York: Morrow Junior Books, 1991.

Kinsey-Warnock, Natalie and Helen Kinsey. *The Bear That Heard Crying*. New York: Penguin, 1997.

Kovalski, Maryann. *The Wheels on the Bus*. Boston: Little, Brown & Co., 1987.

LaMarche, Jim. *The Raft*. New York: HarperCollins, 2000.

Laminack, Lester L. *The Sunsets of Miss Olivia Wiggins*. Atlanta: Peachtree, 1998.

Lasky, Kathryn. *Interrupted Journey*. Cambridge: Candlewick Press, 2000.

Lauber, Patricia. *An Octopus Is Amazing*. New York: Crowell, 1990.

Lauture, Denize. *Running the Road to ABC*. New York: Simon & Schuster, 1996.

Lester, Helen. *Listen Buddy*. Boston: Houghton Mifflin, 1995.

Levinson, Riki. *Watch the Stars Come Out*. New York: Dutton Children's Books, 1985.

Lindbergh, Reeve. *The Day the Goose Got Loose.* New York: Penguin Putnam Books for Young Readers, 1995.

Lionni, Leo. *A Flea Story.* New York: Scholastic, 1977.

Lobel, Arnold. *Ming Lo Moves the Mountain.* New York: Greenwillow Books, 1982.

Lowell, Susan. *The Three Little Javelinas.* New York: Scholastic, 1992.

Lowry, Lois. *Number the Stars.* Boston: Houghton Mifflin, 1989.

Lyon, George Ella. *Come a Tide.* New York: Orchard Books, 1993.

MacLachlan, Patricia. *All the Places to Love.* New York: HarperCollins, 1994.

MacLachlan, Patricia. *Sarah Plain and Tall.* New York: Harper & Row, 1985.

MacLachlan, Patricia. *Sick Day.* New York: Doubleday Book for Young Readers, 2001.

MacLachlan, Patricia. *Through Grandpa's Eyes.* New York: HarperCollins, 1980.

Manson, Ainslie, and Dean Griffiths. *Ballerinas Don't Wear Glasses.* Victoria, BC: Orca Book Publishers, 2000.

Marshak, Suzanna. *I Am the Ocean.* New York: Little, Brown, 1991.

Marshall, James. *Goldilocks and the Three Bears.* New York: Dial Books, 1988.

Marshall, James. *The Three Little Pigs.* New York: Dial Books for Young Readers, 1989.

Marshall, Rita. *I Hate to Read.* Mankato, MN: Creative Editions, 1992.

Martin, Bill Jr. *Brown Bear, Brown Bear, What Do You See?* New York: Henry Holt & Co. 1992.

Martin, Bill Jr. *Chicka Chicka Boom Boom.* New York: Simon & Schuster, 1989.

Martin, Bill Jr. *Knots on a Counting Rope.* New York: Henry Holt, 1987.

Martin, Rafe. *The Rough Face Girl.* New York: G.P. Putnam's Sons, 1992.

Mathis, Sharon Bell. *Sidewalk Story.* New York: Viking Penguin, 1971.

McCloskey, Robert. *Make Way for Ducklings.* New York: Viking Press, 1969.

McFarland, Lyn Rossiter. *Widget.* New York: Farrar Straus Giroux, 2001.

McGovern, Ann. *Stone Soup.* New York: Scholastic, 1968.

McPhail, David. *Edward and the Pirates.* Boston: Little, Brown and Company, 1997.

Miles, Miska. *Annie and the Old One.* Boston: Little, Brown & Company, 1971.

Miller, William. *Richard Wright and the Library Card.* New York: Lee & Low Books, 1997.

Morgan, Pierr. *The Turnip.* New York: Philomel Books, 1990.

Mosel, Arlene. *Tikki Tikki Tembo.* New York: Henry Holt, 1989.

Most, Bernard. *Pets in Trumpets.* San Diego: Harcourt Brace Jovanovich, 1991.

Most, Bernard. *There's an Ant in Anthony.* New York: Mulberry Books, 1980.

Munsch, Robert. *Aaron's Hair.* New York: Scholastic, 2000.

Munsch, Robert. *Andrew's Loose Tooth.* New York: Scholastic, 1998.

Munsch, Robert. *Mortimer.* Toronto: Annick Press, 1985.

Naylor, Phyllis Reynolds. *Shiloh.* New York: Antheneum, 1991.

Numeroff, Laura. *If You Give a Mouse a Cookie.* New York: HarperCollins, 1985.

O'Brien, Robert C. *Mrs. Frisby and the Rats of NIMH.* New York: Antheneum, 1971.

O'Dell, Scott. *Island of the Blue Dolphins.* Boston: Houghton Mifflin, 1960.

Olson, Mary W. *Nice Try, Tooth Fairy.* New York: Simon & Schuster, 2000.

O'Neill, Mary. *Hailstones and Halibut Bones.* New York: Bantam Doubleday Dell, 1961.

Oppenheim, Ruth. *Fireflies for Nathan*. New York: Puffin Books, 1996.

Pallotta, Jerry. *Dory Story*. Watertown, MA: Charlesbridge, 2000.

Parrish, Peggy. *Amelia Bedelia*. New York: HarperCollins, 1963.

Paterson, Katherine. *Bridge to Terabithia*. New York: HarperCollins, 1977.

Paulsen, Gary. *Canoe Days*. New York: Doubleday, 1999.

Paulsen, Gary. *Hatchet*. New York: Simon & Schuster, 1987.

Pearson, Susan. *Silver Morning*. San Diego: Harcourt Brace, 1998.

Peek, Merle. *Mary Wore Her Red Dress*. New York: Clarion Books, 1985.

Perrault, Charles. *Cinderella*. New York: Aladdin Books, 1988.

Petach, Heidi. *Goldilocks and the Three Hares*. New York: G.P. Putnam's Sons, 1995.

Pfister, Marcus. *Rainbow Fish*. New York: North-South Books, 1992.

Pinckney, Jerry (adapted by). *The Ugly Duckling*. New York: Morrow Junior Books, 1999.

Polacco, Patricia. *The Bee Tree*. New York: Philomel, 1993.

Polacco, Patricia. *Just Plain Fancy*. New York: Bantam Books, 1990.

Polacco, Patricia. *The Keeping Quilt*. New York: Simon & Schuster, 1988.

Polacco, Patricia. *My Ol' Man*. New York: Philomel Books, 1995.

Polacco, Patricia. *My Rotten Redheaded Older Brother*. New York: Simon & Schuster, 1994.

Polacco, Patricia. *Thunder Cake*. New York: Philomel Books, 1990.

Potter, Beatrix. *The Tale of Peter Rabbit*. New York: SeaStar Books, 2001.

Rathman, Peggy. *Officer Buckle and Gloria*. New York: Putnam, 1998.

Rawls, Wilson. *Where the Red Fern Grows*. Garden City, NY: Doubleday, 1961.

Ringgold, Faith. *Tar Beach*. New York: Crown Publishers, 1991.

Roberts, Bethany. *Mouse Told His Mother*. Boston: Little, Brown & Co., 1997.

Rosen, Michael. *Rover*. New York: Doubleday Book for Young Readers, 1999.

Ryder, Joanne. *Snail's Spell*. New York: Puffin Books, 1982.

Rylant, Cynthia. *An Angel for Solomon Singer*. New York: Orchard Books, 1992.

Rylant, Cynthia. *Bookshop Dog*. New York: Scholastic, 1996.

Rylant, Cynthia. *Cookie Store Cat*. New York: Scholastic, 1999.

Rylant, Cynthia. *The Great Gracie Chase*. New York: Blue Sky Press, 2001.

Rylant, Cynthia. *Henry and Mudge: The First Book*. New York: Simon & Schuster, 1987.

Rylant, Cynthia. *The Relatives Came*. New York: Macmillan, 1985.

Rylant, Cynthia. *When I Was Young in the Mountains*. New York: Aladdin Books, 1991.

Sayre, April Pulley. *Turtle, Turtle, Watch Out!* New York: Orchard Books, 2000.

Sendak, Maurice. *Chicken Soup with Rice*. New York: Harper & Row, 1962.

Shannon, David. *David Goes to School*. New York: Blue Sky Press, 1999.

Slangerup, Erik Jon. *Dirt Boy*. Morton Grove, IL: Albert Whitman & Company, 2000.

Slobodkina, Esphyr. *Caps for Sale*. New York: HarperCollins, 1968.

Smith, Robert Kimmell. *War with Grandpa*. New York: Delacorte Press, 1984.

Speare, Elizabeth George. *Sign of the Beaver*. Boston: Houghton Mifflin, 1983.

Spinelli, Jerry. *Wringer*. New York: HarperCollins, 1997.

Steptoe, John. *Mufaro's Beautiful Daughters*. New York: Lothrop, Lee & Shepard Books, 1987.

Stevens, Janet. *My Big Dog*. New York: Golden Book, 1999.

Stevens, Janet. *Tops and Bottoms*. San Diego: Harcourt Brace, 1995.

Stevenson, James. *Grandpa's Too Good Garden*. New York: Greenwillow, 1989.

Stevenson, James. *Rolling Rose*. New York: Greenwillow, 1992.

Stewart, Sarah. *The Gardener*. New York: Farrar, Straus & Giroux, 1997.

Stewart, Sarah. *The Library*. New York: Farrar, Straus & Giroux, 1995.

Stolz, Mary. *Storm in the Night*. New York: HarperCollins, 1988.

Swanson, Susan Marie. *Letter to the Lake*. New York: DK Publishing, 1998.

Sweeny, Joan. *Me on the Map*. New York: Crown Publishers, 1996.

Taback, Simms (retold by). *There Was an Old Lady Who Swallowed a Fly*. New York: Viking, 1997.

Turner, Ann. *Dakota Dugout*. New York: Simon & Schuster, 1985.

Turner, Ann. *Nettie's Trip South*. New York: Macmillan, 1987.

Van Allsburg, Chris. *Jumanji*. Boston: Houghton Mifflin, 1981.

Van Laan, Nancy. *Possum Come A-Knockin'*. New York: Alfred A. Knopf, 1990.

Viorst, Judith. *Alexander and the Terrible, Horrible, No Good, Very Bad Day*. New York: Antheneum Books, 1972.

Viorst, Judith. *Earrings!* New York: Antheneum Books, 1990.

Waber, Bernard. *Ira Sleeps Over*. New York: Houghton Mifflin, 1975.

Waddell, Martin. *Owl Babies*. Cambridge, MA: Candlewick Press, 1992.

Wargin, Kathy-Jo. *Legend of the Loon*. Chelsea, MI: Sleeping Bear Press, 2000.

Wells, Rosemary. *Bunny Money*. New York: Dial Books, 1997.

Wells, Rosemary. *Max's Dragon Shirt*. New York: Penguin Putnam Books for Young Readers, 1997.

Wells, Rosemary. *Noisy Nora*. New York: Dial Books, 1997.

Whatley, Bruce. *Looking for Crabs*. Sydney: HarperCollins, 1992.

White, E. B. *Charlotte's Web*. New York: Harper & Row, 1952.

White, Ruth. *Bell Prater's Boy*. New York: Farrar Strauss & Giroux, 1996.

Williams, Margery. *Velveteen Rabbit*. New York: Doubleday & Co., 1975.

Williams, Suzanne. *Library Lil*. New York: Penguin, 1997.

Williams, Vera. *A Chair for My Mother*. New York: Greenwillow Books, 1982.

Willis, Jeanne. *Earthlets as Explained by Professor Xargle*. New York: Penguin, 1988.

Wood, Audrey. *Quick as a Cricket*. New York: Child's Play, International, 1982.

Wood, Don and Audrey Wood. *The Little Mouse, the Red Ripe Strawberry, and the Big Hungry Bear*. New York: Child's Play International, 1990.

Wood, Douglas. *A Quiet Place*. New York: Simon & Schuster, 2002.

Woodson, Jacqueline. *The Other Side*. New York: G. P. Putnam's Sons, 2001.

Yolen, Jane. *Letting Swift River Go*. Boston: Little, Brown & Co., 1992.

Yolen, Jane. *Owl Moon*. New York: Philomel Books, 1987.

Young, Ed. *Seven Blind Mice*. New York: Philomel Books, 1992.

Zolotow, Charlotte. *The Storm Book*. New York: HarperCollins, 1952.

Professional Resources

Allington, Richard L. "The Schools We Have. The Schools We Need." *The Reading Teacher* 48 (1994), 2-16.

Allington, Richard L. *What Really Matters for Struggling Readers*. New York: Addison Wesley Longman, 2001.

Allington, Richard L., and Patricia M. Cunningham. *Schools That Work: Where All Children Read and Write*. New York: HarperCollins, 1996.

Anderson, Richard C., et.al. *Becoming a Nation of Readers*. Washington, DC: Center for the Study of Reading, 1985.

Atwell, Nancie. *In the Middle: New Understandings About Writing, Reading, and Learning*, 2d ed. Portsmouth, NH: Heinemann, 1998.

Atwell, Nancie. *In the Middle: Writing, Reading, and Learning with Adolescents*. Portsmouth, NH: Boynton/Cook, 1987.

Avery, Carol. *…And with a Light Touch*. Portsmouth, NH: Heinemann, 1993.

Calkins, Lucy McCormick. *The Art of Teaching Reading*. New York: Addison Wesley Longman, 2001.

Clay, Marie M. *An Observation Survey of Early Literacy Achievement*. Portsmouth, NH: Heinemann, 1993.

Cunningham, Patricia M., and Richard L. Allington. *Classrooms That Work*, 2d ed. New York: Longman, 1999.

Fiderer, Adele. *35 Rubrics & Checklists to Assess Reading and Writing*. New York: Scholastic Professional Books, 1998.

Fiderer, Adele. *40 Rubrics and Checklists to Assess Reading and Writing*. New York: Scholastic Professional Books, 1999.

Fiderer, Adele. *Practical Assessments for Literature-Based Reading Classrooms*. New York: Scholastic Professional Books, 1995.

Fountas, Irene C., and Gay Su Pinnell. *Guided Reading: Good First Teaching for All Children*. Portsmouth, NH: Heinemann, 1996.

Fountas, Irene C., and Gay Su Pinnell. *Guiding Readers and Writers, Grades 3-6*. Portsmouth, NH: Heinemann, 2001.

Harvey, Stephanie, and Anne Goudvis. *Strategies That Work: Teaching Comprehension to Enhance Understanding*. York, ME: Stenhouse, 2000.

Hindley, Joanne. *In the Company of Children*. York, ME: Stenhouse, 1996.

Keene, Ellin Oliver, and Susan Zimmermann. *Mosaic of Thought*. Portsmouth, NH: Heinemann, 1997.

Pearson, P. David, L.R. Roehler, J.A. Dole, and G.G. Duffy. "Developing Expertise in Reading Comprehension." In *What Research Has to Say About Reading Instruction: What Should Be Taught and How Should It Be Taught?* 2d ed. J. Farstrup and S.J. Samuels, eds. Newark, DE: International Reading Association, 1992.

Robb, Laura. *Easy-to-Manage Reading and Writing Conferences*. New York: Scholastic Professional Books, 1998.

Robb, Laura. *Teaching Reading in Middle School*. New York: Scholastic Professional Books, 2000.

Routman, Regie. *Conversations*. Portsmouth, NH: Heinemann, 2000.

Shea, Mary. *Taking Running Records*. New York: Scholastic Professional Books, 2000.

Taberski, Sharon. *On Solid Ground: Strategies for Teaching Reading K–3*. Portsmouth, NH: Heinemann, 2000.

Trelease, Jim. *The Read-Aloud Handbook*. New York: Penguin Books, 1995.

Wilde, Sandra. *Miscue Analysis Made Easy: Building on Student Strengths*. Portsmouth, NH: Heinemann, 2000.

Story Chats

Book Title _____

Author _____

Before meeting with your group:

    📖 Note things you want to discuss (you can use sticky notes).

    📖 Write down any confusing parts (or use sticky notes).

    📖 Write questions you want to ask the group.

Are you prepared for your Story Chat?

    ☐ I have read the book (or the assigned part).

    ☐ I have noted things to discuss.

    ☐ I have noted confusing parts.

    ☐ I have questions to ask the group.

One thing we need to discuss in our Story Chat is:

_____

_____

_____

These were things I was confused about:

    1. _____

    2. _____

    3. _____

Here are questions I will ask:

    1. _____

    2. _____

    3. _____

    4. _____

    5. _____

Name _____ Date _____

After the Story Chat

Three things that I learned or were helpful from the Story Chat:

1. _____

_____

2. _____

_____

3. _____

_____

These are things we should do differently for our next meeting:

_____

_____

_____

Our next assignment is: _____

Semester End Reading Inventory

Knowing what to read...

How do you select a "just right" book? How do you know it is a "just right book"?
Can you give an example of a "just right book"?

_____

_____

_____

_____

Knowing how to read...

How many reading strategies can you think of? Can you tell how you use each one?

Strategy name...	How I can use it...

Revisiting the Reading Workshop: Management, Mini-Lessons, and Strategies • Scholastic Professional Books

Knowing what to look for...

How many story elements can you list?

_____

_____

What are some things that good authors do in their writing?

_____

_____

_____

What was your favorite read aloud this year? Tell why you liked it.

_____

_____

_____

What was the best book you read to yourself? Tell why you liked it.

_____

_____

_____

How have you become a better reader?

_____

_____

_____

What is one goal for yourself as a reader?

_____

_____

_____

_____

Reading Workshop Mini-Lesson Topics*

MINI-LESSON TOPIC	Introduced	Reviewed	Reviewed	Notes/Related Literature
Workshop Procedures				
Workshop introduction/procedures/rules				
Appropriate workshop voices				
Listening skills				
Reading with a partner/group				
Book choice—appropriate difficulty/variety				
Choosing a "book nook"				
Book abandonment				
Reading conference—teacher's role/student's role				
Reading folder/log/journal				
Take-home book/homework journal				
Book talks				
Strategic Reading				
Previewing a book				
Setting a purpose for reading				
Making predictions				
Applying "fix-up" strategies to comprehension problems				
Reflecting on reading				
Visualizing				
Questioning				
Making inferences				
Drawing conclusions				
Comparing and contrasting texts				

* This form provides a start for you as you create your own record sheet of mini-lesson topics covered in your Workshop. You can use what's here for these specific topics and/or create a blank version for all the other topics that you cover during the year. (Remember, this list is just a start and not comprehensive.)